THE
ADVANCED
ROBLOX CODING
═══ BOOK ═══
AN UNOFFICIAL GUIDE

Learn How to Script Games,
Code Objects and Settings, and
Create Your Own World!

HEATH HASKINS
(a.k.a. CodePrime8)

Adams Media
New York   London   Toronto   Sydney   New Delhi

I would like to dedicate this book to my family: my wife, Elizabeth, and my two children, Hope and Oliver, who have supported, inspired, and pushed me into being who I am today.

I would also like to dedicate this book to every child, and every parent of a child with a special need, reminding you that what others call a disability may in fact be your superpower. Don't let anyone tell you that you can't be something you want to be.

▲adamsmedia

Adams Media
An Imprint of Simon & Schuster, Inc.
57 Littlefield Street
Avon, Massachusetts 02322

First Adams Media trade paperback edition March 2019

ADAMS MEDIA and colophon are trademarks of Simon & Schuster.

For information about special discounts for bulk purchases, please contact Simon & Schuster Special Sales at 1-866-506-1949 or business@simonandschuster.com.

The Simon & Schuster Speakers Bureau can bring authors to your live event. For more information or to book an event contact the Simon & Schuster Speakers Bureau at 1-866-248-3049 or visit our website at www.simonspeakers.com.

Interior design by Colleen Cunningham

Manufactured in the United States of America

Printed by LSC Communications, Harrisonburg, VA, U.S.A.
10 9 8 7 6 5 4 3

Library of Congress Cataloging-in-Publication Data has been applied for.

ISBN 978-1-72140-007-2
ISBN 978-1-72140-008-9 (ebook)

CONTENTS

INTRODUCTION

I'm sure you are already pretty good at playing Roblox games. You may have wondered how the game maker created the sword you have, or the pets that follow you, and maybe even have a little bit of knowledge about the development environment in Roblox Studio, which is the application you use to make games to play in the Roblox world. But have you wanted to know how to:

- Teleport a character?
- Keep track of a player's inventory?
- Make a customized leaderboard that matches up with your specific game?
- Write your own code when Roblox doesn't have a specific script you want?

You'll learn all that, and a bunch more, in *The Advanced Roblox Coding Book*. We'll make it all happen using Roblox's version of the Lua coding language. (Don't worry, writing code is actually not that hard!)

I'll break down the basics of coding in easy-to-understand examples that you can use right away in your games. After you see how my examples work, you'll be able to use your imagination to add your own style to them. Before you know it, your games will be so much fun that people will want to play them again and again!

Here's what you'll learn in this book:

- **The basics of Lua scripting:** you'll become familiar with code itself and will learn what the basic structure of code looks like.
- **The power of coding with "variables," "loops," and "conditionals":** several simple Lua features that can help your game execute tons of commands.
- **Tricks for managing player health:** you have many options for player health, from giving a character more power to taking it all away.
- **Moving characters around within your game:** learn different techniques for teleporting players.
- **How to save player data:** set up a scoreboard and save information from one playing session to the next.
- **The steps for creating a game, from start to finish:** you'll learn how to brainstorm your game concept, identify what codes you'll need, and use programming to accomplish your goals.
- **Important security measures:** it's essential to protect your games as you create them.

The great thing about making games for Roblox is that it gives you the freedom to create almost any game you can imagine. Once you understand coding, nothing will hold you back. Whether you just want to fool around with Roblox Studio on the weekends or become a professional video game creator some-day, *The Advanced Roblox Coding Book* will start you off on the right foot. Let's get coding!

START WITH THE BASICS

FOR BEGINNER INFORMATION ON HOW TO GET STARTED PLAYING ROBLOX, CHECK *THE ULTIMATE ROBLOX BOOK: AN UNOFFICIAL GUIDE* BY DAVID JAGNEAUX. THIS BOOK CONTAINS A LOT OF INFORMATION ABOUT ROBLOX, BUT IT'S NOT A DEFINITIVE GUIDE ON ABSOLUTELY EVERY NOOK AND CRANNY OF THE ENTIRE GAME. LIKE ANY GOOD GAME MAKER, THE FOLKS WHO MAKE ROBLOX ARE ALWAYS ADDING NEW FEATURES AND WAYS TO PLAY, SO IT'S IMPOSSIBLE FOR A SINGLE BOOK TO COVER EVERYTHING.

THIS BOOK WILL ALSO NOT INCLUDE ANY "GET RICH QUICK" SCHEMES FOR MAKING LOTS OF MONEY (ROBUX) QUICKLY OR FOR HOW TO BECOME RICH OFF OF CREATING AND SELLING THINGS IN ROBLOX. NO MATTER WHAT YOU READ OR SEE ON THE INTERNET, THE ONLY WAY TO MAKE MONEY IN ROBLOX IS THROUGH HARD WORK, CREATIVITY, AND DEDICATION. THAT'S IT.

PART 1

NOOB

CHAPTER

1

THE VERY BASIC

This chapter will go over how to use the Roblox Studio program to manage scripts, and how to recognize and write some very basic coding. I know, I know, this beginner information is not always the most exciting, but we gotta get it under our belts before we can move on to the fun stuff.

LOADING STUDIO

I'm going to assume that you already have a Roblox account. (If you need a rundown of how to set one up, grab *The Ultimate Roblox Book: An Unofficial Guide*.) Log in and let's get step 1 out of the way: open Studio.

Roblox Corporation
LOOK FOR THIS ICON TO OPEN STUDIO.

There are two ways you can open Studio:

1. On Windows, go to Start, then Roblox. You should get two icons. Click on the blue icon labeled Roblox Studio.
2. Go to www.roblox.com, log in, and head to the Create tab. Click on Create New Game and select either a template or baseplate option, then click Create Game.

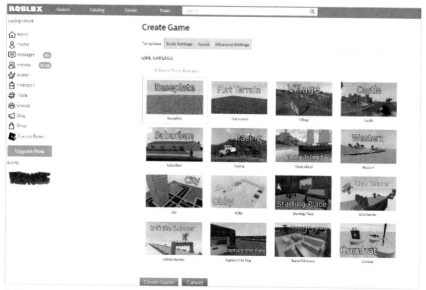

Roblox Corporation

THE CREATE GAME SCREEN.

(You can also open Studio by selecting a game you have already created, then Edit from its Context menu.)

KNOW YOUR GAME SETTINGS

AS OF MID-2018 BY DEFAULT YOUR GAME SETTING IS PRIVATE (MEANING THE GENERAL PUBLIC CAN'T SEE IT UNLESS YOU INVITE THEM TO), AND EXPERIMENTAL MODE IS ON (MEANING CLIENT-SIDE CHANGES AFFECT EVERYONE). WE WILL CHANGE THESE SETTINGS LATER.

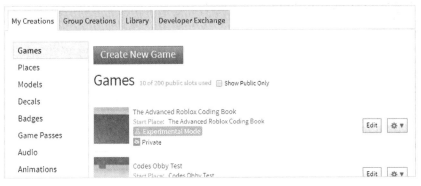

Roblox Corporation
YOU SHOULD NOW SEE YOUR GAME.

Now that the game has been created, it will appear in your list of My Creations. Click on Edit to start up Studio.

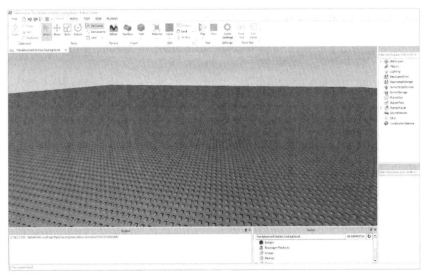

Roblox Corporation
THE STUDIO SETUP SHOULD LOOK SOMETHING LIKE THIS.

Your Studio may have a different layout. I have changed mine around to the way I like to use it. You can leave the windows in the default layout, or customize the layout to make it easier for you to use. Most windows can be dragged around inside the studio environment or pulled out completely. If you would like to hide or show a window, you can do so from the View tab at the top.

WHAT IS A SCRIPT?

A script is a set of instructions to perform specific tasks in a certain way. For example, you may want your character to drink a potion that makes them regain hit points, or hit a dragon with a sword so the dragon loses hit points. Those things happen thanks to a script that the Roblox creators wrote and embedded in the program. Before I explain more, here are a couple of terms you should know:

- **Server:** A server is the central place an online game is stored and runs from.
- **Client:** A client is the program that allows you to connect to the server. Through it, you can see and interact with the server and other players.

When you play a Roblox game, a server at Roblox is responsible for running the game. When you connect to the game server, your computer opens up a client to show you what is actually a copy of the game. The server and each client talk to each other to keep the game running smoothly for everyone.

SCRIPT LOCATIONS

There are two kinds of script:

- A **local script** will run on a user's client (meaning, on their computer).
- A **server script** (usually just called a **script**) will run on the Roblox server that is running the game (meaning, in a remote location).

The script location is important because where the script is located will determine what the script can change. Games in Roblox have something called Experimental Mode. If Experimental Mode is on and a local script makes changes to a game, those changes get passed to the server. The server then passes those changes on to all the other clients (players) connected to the game.

Now say Timmy comes along and he has an Exploit, a malicious program to cheat with, that allows him to inject his own script into your game. Unfortunately, Timmy's code makes a VERY inappropriate song start playing in the game. When the server gets this change, it will tell everyone else's game to start playing that song as well. Yep, your game has just been compromised.

When Experimental Mode is turned off, you can no longer make direct changes to the server through the local scripts. When Timmy now starts the song, it will only happen on his client. It will not replicate that change to anyone else.

To turn Experimental Mode off:

1. In the Explorer window, click on Workspace.

Roblox Corporation
LOOK FOR THE WORK-SPACE OPTION.

2. In the Properties window, check Filtering Enabled.

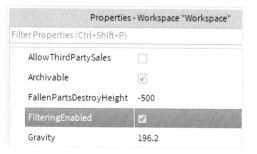

Roblox Corporation
IT'S IMPORTANT TO CHECK THIS BOX TO BE SURE YOUR GAME IS SET UP CORRECTLY.

STARTING A SCRIPT

First, let's add a script into your Workspace, which is the first object you'll see in the Explorer window on the right side of the screen. For example, say we have a door that we want to open and close when someone clicks on the handle. We would place the script directly into the Part we create to represent the door, using it as a container for our script. But what if we wanted to make the sunrise move across the sky, set in the evening, then add the moon? To control the time of day like that, we could place a script directly into the Workspace. The process is the same for all scripts. (We will work with a server script to get used to the basics for now, and revisit local scripts later on in the book.) To begin a script, click on the Plus symbol next to Workspace.

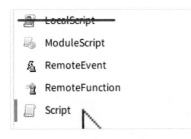

Roblox Corporation
CLICK ON THIS PLUS ICON TO START TO CREATE SCRIPTS.

Type *script* into the search box.

Roblox Corporation
SEARCH FOR SCRIPT.

Select the Script object, shown with a blank scroll icon.

Roblox Corporation
BE SURE YOU CHOOSE SCRIPT.

LocalScript

ModuleScript

RemoteEvent

RemoteFunction

Script

Note: make sure you do *not* add the LocalScript.

After adding the script, your Studio layout should look similar to this:

Roblox Corporation
HERE'S WHAT YOU'LL SEE WITH A SCRIPT WINDOW OPEN.

If the text in the scripting window is too small, hold down CTRL (Command on Mac) and use your scroll wheel to zoom in.

WRITING SOME CODE

Type in these words (the colors change as you type them):

```
print("Hello, world!")
```

"Hello, world!" is the simplest script anyone can write—that's why it's the first program people usually write in any programming language. The same goes for Lua. Once you have it typed in, you can press F5 to run the program, or you can click on the Play button from the Test menu at the top of the screen. You will see "Hello, world!" in the output box at the bottom of your screen.

CHAPTER

2

VARIABLES

The "Hello, world!" script might be easy to write, but it's not very useful or exciting. What we need to make scripts much more interesting is a "variable." We'll use variables to store, change, and manage data in your scripts.

WHAT IS A VARIABLE?

A variable is a container for some kind of data that is relevant to your game. The data represented by a variable is called its "value." Values are often called "arguments." There are several types of data that you can use in your scripts.

LUA IS SMART WITH DATA TYPES

OTHER COMPUTER PROGRAMMING LANGUAGES (SUCH AS C# OR JAVA) REQUIRE THAT YOU FIRST TELL THE PROGRAM WHAT TYPE OF DATA A VARIABLE WILL BE HOLDING. FOR EXAMPLE, YOU HAVE TO TELL THE PROGRAM THAT A PARTICULAR VARIABLE WILL BE HOLDING A NUMBER. LUA IS REALLY GOOD ABOUT KNOWING WHAT YOU MEAN, SO IT'S NOT A SEPARATE STEP IN THE PROCESS.

DATA TYPES

What kind of information you store inside a variable is called its data type. Even though we don't have to tell Lua what kind of data type our variable is going to be, it's important to know what kinds of data types you can use. The following table lists the data type, an example, a description of what can be stored, and common ways you'll use that particular data type.

DATA TYPE	EXAMPLES	DESCRIPTION	COMMON USES IN ROBLOX GAMES
String	"Hello, world!"	Strings represent text, such as words or sentences, including letters, numbers and punctuation. String values are surrounded by quotation marks.	To make characters "talk."
Number	42 3.14159 -3.0	Numbers represent numerical values, which can be used to hold counts, perform mathematical equations, and represent units of measure.	Hit points, amounts of money, timers.
Table	{apple = "red", banana = "yellow", pear = "green"}	Tables represent pairs of items. The first item in a pair is called the "index" or "key." The second item in a pair is called its "value." In the example to the left, the keys are types of fruit, and the values are their colors. Tables are declared with brackets, like these: {}.	A complex object, like a vehicle, or a list of items and their properties.

DATA TYPE	EXAMPLES	DESCRIPTION	COMMON USES IN ROBLOX GAMES
Userdata	game.Workspace	Userdata is a pointer, or reference to an object. The Userdata doesn't contain information itself, but points to an object.	Working with special objects, like the Workspace.
Boolean	true, false	A single value of 1 or 0. True or False. Used in logic.	Whether or not a player has defeated a boss.
Nil	nil	A special type that indicates that no value has been assigned.	Creating variables in advance, before you know what they will contain.
Function	print(), tostring(), tonumber()	A function is a set of instructions that have been grouped together and given a name. Instead of writing the same instructions multiple times, you can group them into a function, then "call" the function to execute those instructions whenever you want. There is a special kind of function called a "method." Methods perform an action on a variable.	Printing things, defining how an object behaves.

NAMING VARIABLES

You'll want to name your variables right off the bat so you can remember what information is being stored there. You can name a variable almost anything you like.

Here are some examples of naming a variable:

```
NAME of variable = VALUE of that variable
LifeAnswer = 42
DogSound = "Bork Bork"
smallTable = {1,2,3}
WSpace = game.Workspace
CanRun = true
mixedTable = {42,"Bork Bork",{1,2,3},game.Workspace,true,
print}
```

Here are some guidelines for how to name a variable (the left side of the equation):

- You cannot start a variable with a number, like 1cat, or 3dog. You *can* use a number after a name is given, like Cat1 or Dog3.
- Do not name a variable the same as a function name, such as **print**, **type**, or **error**. For example, you could type **print** = 13. This will break the **print** function, so the next time you type **print**("Hello, world!") your script will crash.
- Don't be afraid to use long names. In the past, programmers would shorten their code by shortening the variable names. Let's say a programmer had a variable like "The Smallest Book Title Cover." He or she might have

made a variable named "smBKTCov." This is confusing, especially if you are working with a group of programmers, or if you have to revisit the code after not looking at it for a long time. Make your variables mean something. There is no harm in having a longer name.

PLAYING WITH STRINGS

Strings are very useful when you're writing code—they will provide dialogue, names, and item descriptions.

Let's go back to our sample script from the end of Chapter 1. Let's delete **print**("Hello, world!") and instead create a variable called MyFirstName and give it the string value of our name. Then, let's create a second variable and call it MyLastName.

```
MyFirstName = "Heath"
MyLastName = "Haskins"
```

Let's use the **print** function to make our script show us our new variables along with some text. We'll put the text in quotes to make it a string. We will use commas to separate the string from the variables we just created (MyFirstName and MyLastName).

```
print("Good Evening", MyFirstName, MyLastName)
```

Double-check the spelling of your text. When you are ready, press F5 to run your game.

PUTTING STRINGS TOGETHER

Instead of using commas in the **print** function, you can combine (or "concatenate" in computer programming language) strings by using two periods. Let's create another variable called `FullProperName`, by concatenating the two variables, and some separation string (the space and comma within the quotes).

```
FullProperName = MyLastName .. ", " .. MyFirstName
print(FullProperName)
```

STRING OPERATIONS

String variables have several built-in methods attached to them, such as:

- Making all the letters uppercase.
- Making all the letters lowercase.
- Getting the length of the string.
- Pulling out a specific part of the string.

Type in the following code. Lines 2–6 each use the built-in string function, known as a method, by calling them directly on the variable.

CODE	WHAT IT DOES
`myString = "I'm a programmer"`	This line creates a variable called `myString`. Because `myString` is a string data type, it inherits special methods for working with its value.
`print(myString:upper())`	This is the `:upper()` method. This will convert all the characters in the string from lowercase to uppercase.
`print(myString:lower())`	This is the `:lower()` method, which is just the opposite of upper. It makes all of the characters lowercase.
`print(myString: sub(6,15))`	`:sub()` stands for substring. It will return a part of the string, and takes two arguments when called as a method. The first argument is what position in the string to start, and the second argument is what position to end. If we were to count our string's characters, then "I" would be one, "m" would be two, the first space would be three, and so on. We start at position 6 "p" and go to position 15 "r." If you are using the `string.sub()` method, it will take three arguments. The first is what you want to get the substring for, second is start position, and third is end position.
`print(myString: reverse())`	This reverses the string value so that it is backward.
`print(myString:len())`	This line will make the script print out the length of the string (e.g., how many characters are in the string).

There are two ways to call a type's methods in Lua: via a variable (by using a ":") or via the type itself (by using a "."). Say we had a string variable defined like this:

```
dog_name = "Buster"
```

These two lines would print the same thing:

```
print(dog_name:upper())
print(string.upper(dog_name))
```

This applies to all of the type's methods, such as lower, reverse, and len, in the case of the string type. Calling via the variable, as in the first case above, is more concise, so you may find it easier to read. This table shows both ways of calling these methods.

CALL VIA VARIABLE	CALL VIA TYPE
print(myString:upper())	print(string.upper(myString))
print(myString:lower())	print(string.lower(myString))
print(myString:sub(6,15))	print(string.sub(myString,6,15))
print(myString:reverse())	print(string.reverse(myString))
print(myString:len())	print(string.len(myString))

PLAYING WITH NUMBERS

Let's move on to numbers. Addition, Subtraction, Multiplication, and Division are the basics. However, these are not the only things we can do. The math in Lua can get really complicated, really quick, and these operations will cover most of the scenarios you'll run into when coding. We use different symbols to represent the different operations we want to perform. The table below shows what symbols to use.

OPERATION	SYMBOL	EXAMPLE	WHAT IT DOES
Addition	+	1 + 1 = 2	Adds two numbers together.
Subtraction	–	10 - 5 = 5	Subtracts second number from first number.
Multiplication	*	2 * 2 = 4	Multiplies two numbers.
Division	/	10 / 5 = 2	Divides first number by second number.
Modulus	%	5 % 2 = 1	Returns the remainder of division.
Exponent	^	10 ^ 2 = 100	Takes first number to the power of second.
Negate	-\<var\>	Var = -10 -Var = 10	Also called Unary, same as * -1, will reverse the sign of a number or variable.

It's important to remember the order of operations when working with math. Order of operations refers to the steps you take when solving an equation. The acronym PEDMAS describes the order in which to do the steps: Parentheses, Exponents, Division/Multiplication, and then finally Addition/Subtraction. For example, 1 + 2 * 3 = 7 is correct, but 1 + 2 * 3 = 9 is not correct.

We can test all of these out by assigning some variables, then printing out the different operations results.

X = 10
Y = 5

CODE EXAMPLE	RESULT
`print(X + Y)`	15
`print(X - Y)`	5
`print(X * Y)`	50
`print(X / Y)`	2
`print(X % Y)`	0
`print(X ^ Y)`	100,000
`print(-X, -Y)`	-10, -5

COMPLEX MATHEMATICS

Depending on the type of game you're making, you may need complex mathematics. For example, if you're creating a strategy game where computer-controlled characters need to automatically find the best path from one point to the other, you'll need to work with graphs. This concept lies outside the problem-solving of PEDMAS. If you find you do need to perform more complex mathematics, you will need to use Roblox's math library. To see what the math library has to offer, type **math** followed by a period. You should get a list of all available math functions.

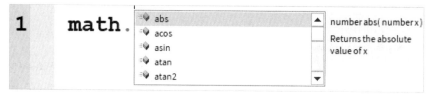

Roblox Corporation

THERE ARE LOTS OF MATH FUNCTIONS YOU COULD USE.

The math library contains functions that will take in one or more arguments and return the calculated values. For example, the `abs` function will take one argument and return the absolute value of that argument.

Let's use another math keyword to return the value of pi. This can be used to get a more precise calculation, giving you twelve more decimal points than the commonly used representation of pi, which is 3.14.

```
print(math.pi)
```

LEARNING LOGIC

Logic is the comparison of values, which returns either a true or false statement. Logic is usually made of two items:

1. Comparison operators, which check the values of numbers (or other objects) and return a true or false.
2. Logic operators, which are used to check if two or more comparison results evaluate to true.

Let's take a deeper look at the different operators and try some examples.

COMPARISON OPERATORS
This table outlines some common comparison operators which you might use when determining if a player has enough money to buy something.

OPERATOR	EQUATION	HOW TO EVALUATE TRUE OR FALSE
Equal to	A == B	1 == 1 true 0 == 1 false
Less than	A < B	0 < 1 true 1 < 0 false
Less than or Equal to	A <= B	1 <= 1 true 1 <= 0 false
Greater than	A > B	1 > 0 true 0 > 1 false
Greater than or Equal to	A >= B	1 >= 1 true 0 >= 1 false
Not equal to	A ~= B	1 ~= 0 true 1 ~= 1 false

LOGIC OPERATORS

Here're more operators to help you evaluate multiple options.

OPERATOR	EVALUATION	HOW TO EVALUATE TRUE OR FALSE
and	A and B	false and false returns false true and false returns false false and true returns false true and true returns true
or	A or B	false or false returns false true or false returns true false or true returns true true or true returns true
not	not A not (A and B)	returns the opposite of true or false not true returns false

Logic statements are read from left to right. Take the following statement as an example. We've simplified it by simply using the words "false" and "true."

```
if false and true then
    print("worked")
end
```

On the left side of the **and** statement, we have **false**. In order for our **and** statement to return **true**, both the left and right must be true. In this case, the left side was read as false, so the right side is never seen. The statement returns **false** without looking at what was on the right side. The same read order applies in the following **or** statement.

```
if false or true then
    print("worked")
end
```

On the left side of the **or** statement we have **true**. Since the logic for an **or** statement means either side must be true, then this statement is already true, so the right side does not get read or acted on.

MANAGING MULTIPLE LOGIC STATEMENTS AT ONCE

With logic statements, you will find many times that you will use multiple comparisons, joined together. If you need to use more than one logical statement, it's best to put them in parenthesis to keep the logic "nested." Nesting is a way of keeping logic together. Although it looks easier to read with one or two nestings, it will get confusing if you add too many. Here are some examples:

- (5 > 6 or 3 == 3) and (not 5 == 6)
- (false or true) and (true)

COMMENTS AND WHITESPACE

The last bit I would like to cover in this chapter concerns comments and whitespace. They seem like minor details but can actually really help your code stay clear and easy to understand.

COMMENTS

Comments are notes you write to yourself (or anyone else reading your code) to describe exactly what that section of code is doing. Trust me: USE COMMENTS! Write them even if you don't think you will need the notes, and even if it seems like it's just busywork—you'll be surprised by how often you reread them to remind yourself. Comments do not show up anywhere on screen while the game is being played. There are three ways to comment text: single-line comments, multiple-line comments, and long comments.

Most of the time, you will only need to use a single-line comment to explain what's going on in your code. It is good practice to start making comments now, before you get 2,000 lines into the code, and start to realize you don't remember what some of the code is. (Believe me, I've learned this the hard way!) Any type of comment always begins with --. A single-line comment begins with just the --. A multiple-line comment begins with --[[. A long comment begins with --[===[. Here's what they look like in practice.

```
--Single line comment

--[[
   multiple line
   comment.
--]]

--[===[
   Long comment which can also contain [[]] without
   disturbing the comment itself. [====[ and isn't
   affected ]====] by whats inside
--]===]
```

WHITESPACE

Whitespace just refers to the blank lines between lines of code, the spacing between words, and tabs or indents to the code. In Lua, you can have as much whitespace as you like, and I encourage you to space out your code blocks. Put a double enter between functions, and indent your code too. The whitespace does not affect how the code runs, but it makes it much easier to read and check over.

By using the combination of comments and whitespace, your code is going to look more elegant and will be easier to understand.

```lua
function sayhello()              --simple function to say hello
    print("hi there!")          --we print out hello there
end                             --ending the simple function

--complexed function to shutdown server
function EndServer()

    --get list of all players
    lstPlayers = game.Players:GetChildren()

    --loop through our list of players and kick each one.
    for _ ,i in pairs(lstPlayers) do
        i:Kick("The server is shutting down.")
    end
end

sayhello()
wait(5)
EndServer()
```

Just remember, there is no real "right" way of formatting your code. As long as you can understand it, you should be fine. If you really wanted to, you could type out an entire script on one line, and as long as your code is correct, the script will still run properly. That said, in the next image, you will see why we don't do that… It's way too hard to read.

```lua
function sayhello() print("hi there") end function
EndServer() lstPlayers = ...
```

CHAPTER 3

IFS, LOOPS, AND MORE

In this chapter, we will learn about `if` statements and different kinds of loops, such as `for` and `while` statements, and many more logical looping decisions.

THE IF STATEMENT

The first thing we are going to do is take a look at the `if` statement, and start applying the logic we learned in the last chapter. An `if` statement is based on the idea that if a certain condition is met, the code will execute a specific command. If that condition is not met, the code will do something else. The general framework of an `if` statement looks like this:

```
if condition then
    --code goes here
elseif condition2 then
    --code based on something else
else
    --code if no other condition found
end
```

THE IF/THEN STATEMENT

On line 1, we see the way all `if` conditions start: with an `if/then` statement. In order for the code on line 2 to run, the condition on line 1 has to be **true**. Now, what could the condition itself be? It could be something like `MyName == "Heath"`. Now, if your first name happens to be Heath, then this would return **true**, and the code on line 2 would run. But let's pretend your name is not Heath. Then, it would skip ahead to the next condition on line 3.

You might use an `if/then` statement in a game scenario like this: if the player collects a speed power-up, then they will run faster than their default speed.

THE ELSEIF STATEMENT

Let's take a look at line 3. The `elseif` statement is used to evaluate another condition if the one before it turned out to be `false`. If the `elseif` condition is true, then the code on line 4 will run. Let's pretend that the condition for line 3 is `MyName ==` `"Steven"` and that our variable `MyName` is really "Steven." The code on line 4 would run.

NO LIMITS

YOU CAN PUT AS MANY `elseif` STATEMENTS IN THAT YOU LIKE. EACH ONE THAT RETURNS `true` CAUSES THE PROGRAM TO RUN THE CODE THAT FOLLOWS IT.

You might use an `elseif` statement in a game scenario like the previous example, except the player did not pick up the power-up, and therefore would run at their default speed.

THE ELSE STATEMENT

The final statement before we end this block of code is `else`. An `else` statement will run its code when no other condition has come out `true`. This is like the default command. If any of the previous conditions came out to be `true`, this code will get skipped.

The `elseif` and `else` statements are optional. If you have no reason to evaluate them, then you don't have to put them in. A simple `if/then/end` will be enough.

AN EXAMPLE TO TRY

Let's change our code around a little bit, and see how these conditions work with real examples in the code:

```
FirstNumber = 2
SecondNumber = 50

if FirstNumber > SecondNumber then
    print("First Number is Higher")
elseif FirstNumber < SecondNumber then
    print("Second Number is Higher")
else
    print("Numbers are equal?")
end
```

> The Output will read: Second Number is Higher

Now we have given our script some variables (`FirstNumber` and `SecondNumber`) to compare. Once it does that, the code should give us an output of which of those numbers is higher. Here's exactly what the code will do:

- The first **if** statement will run its code only if the first number is greater than the second number.
- The **elseif** statement will run when the second number is greater than the first number.
- Then finally, if the numbers are not greater *or* less than each other, the only logical thing is they are equal.

To get more comfortable with the **if/then**, **elseif**, and **else** commands, change the variables around to the following combinations, and run the script each time to see the different results:

- FirstNumber = 50; SecondNumber = 2
- FirstNumber = 10; SecondNumber = 10
- FirstNumber = "cat"; SecondNumber = 10

The results of the first two will probably be what you expect. The last one, however, will return what is called an *exception* or an error. The warning you get should be "Workspace.Script:3: attempt to compare number with string". We will get to handling exceptions and errors later. For now, you can't compare Numbers to Strings.

WHAT ARE LOOPS?

A loop is a block of code that will run through all of its instructions, then start back at the top and repeat the same instructions until some predetermined condition is set. You might use a loop in a game scenario where you want to keep spawning items like power-ups or monsters at regular intervals.

The main thing to be careful of when dealing with loops is getting stuck in one. In the event a condition is never met, you will enter what's called an infinite loop. No, not like Thanos's glove and the Infinity Stones (although the time stone would be useful for getting more time to code). An infinite loop is just that: infinite. Never-ending. Continuing to run its code until the game shuts down, either because the player leaves or the game crashes, the script is stopped manually or by other sections of code, or someone at Roblox DataCenter spills coffee on the server your game is on. Why did they have coffee inside the server room? I don't know, but at least it stopped your infinite loop!

THE WHILE LOOP

A **while** loop will repeat a block of code until its condition is **false**. Here's an example: While my coffee cup is not full, keep filling it up. Once it is full, stop filling. See? Simple. With a **while** loop, you will need something in the logic statement that gets updated on each loop. That way, you can constantly re-evaluate the condition. For example, with my coffee filling loop, if I am not looking at the cup, I won't know how full it is. Then the coffee will just go over the top, and I'll make a huge mess, and no one wants that.

Let's write code for a **while** statement. We'll add a variable called counter to keep track. You'll notice **do** appears in this script. That is just Lua's way of knowing you've finished spelling out your **while** variable.

```
local counter = 0
while(counter < 10) do
    print(counter)
    counter = counter + 1
end
```

When you run this script, you should get a printout of 0 1 2 3 4 5 6 7 8 9. There are 10 numbers because we started counting at 0, not 1. Our loop ends on 9 because on the last loop, the counter goes from 9 to 10, then checks to see if 10 < 10. This logic is **false**, so the loop ends. If you want to count from

1 to 10, just change your `counter` variable to `= 1`, and the **while** statement to `counter <= 10`. That way, when it starts, it will print out the current value, 1, then increase that value by 1, and continue while `counter` is less than or equal to 10.

THE FOR LOOP

A **for** loop is a counting loop that goes from a starting number to an ending number. You assign a variable to be the placeholder for the current number you are on. These loops work kind of like our **while** loop example, but with a little less code, and a lot more control. A **for** loop needs three arguments:

- Start: the number you want to start counting from.
- End: number you are trying to get to.
- Step: the interval to count by.

What is great about the **for** loop is you can count up, down, or even skip around. Let's see what it commonly looks like. The first line will include your selected numbers in the order outlined above: the number you want to start from, followed by the number you want to stop at, followed by the interval to count by.

```
for x = 1, 10, 1 do
    print(x)
end
```

Running this script gives you the same 1 to 10 count as before. Now let's switch around the numbers and say "Count from 10 to 1." Swap the first 1 and the 10, and change the last number to -1.

```
for x = 10, 1, -1 do
    print(x)
end
```

Now when you run the script, you get a countdown from 10 to 1. Go ahead and change the numbers to 0, 100, 10. This says "Count from 0 to 100, by 10s."

```
for x = 0, 100, 10 do
    print(x)
end
```

In this loop, the count starts at 0. You could change this to 10 if you wanted 10 to be the first number in the loop. If you start your count at 1, then you will get an output of 1, 11, 21, 31... which is not how we wanted to count. Starting at 0 will give you 0, 10, 20, 30...100, which is a nice, even way of counting up by 10s. In all of these examples, the loop will end when the counting reaches the second number.

For example, you might use a **for** loop in a game where you need to count experience points to determine when the player has reached a new level.

THE FOR/IN LOOP

When counting, we normally use numbers. With a **for/in** loop, we can count objects. We can loop over a table data type, and perform a task for each object we find.

Imagine you have a basket full of apples and oranges. This would be your table. We want to go through all of the items in the basket and cut up the apples and peel the oranges. Our statement would be **for** item **in** basket, **do** a certain command. We would add some logic to check if the item was an apple or orange. Let's go ahead and use the example, and make some real code with it. (What? I like apples and oranges!)

```
local basket = {"apple", "apple", "orange", "apple",
"orange", "orange"}

for num, item in pairs(basket) do

    print(num, item)

    if item == "apple" then
        print("cut apple")
    elseif item == "orange" then
        print("peel orange")
    end
end
```

In this code, we have created a table called basket and given it apples and oranges in a mixed-up order. When you create a table like this, each item inside the table has a number. An item inside the table can be referenced by putting the number of that entry after the variable in square brackets. This number is called the key. (You could also call the number the index.) So basket[1] represents the first item in the list, which is an "apple". basket[2] would also be "apple", but basket[3] would be "orange".

Now take a look at the **for** loop we have created. I gave it two variables: num and item. The num variable refers to the key. The item variable refers to the type of fruit. The **pairs** function will return both the num and item variables. The reason we don't just get the same item over and over again is that **pairs** is a special kind of function called an Iterator.

WHAT ARE ITERATORS?

ITERATORS WALK THROUGH A SET OF ITEMS, AND KEEP TRACK OF WHICH ITEM WAS RETURNED LAST. EVERY TIME YOU CALL AN ITERATOR, IT MOVES ON TO THE NEXT ITEM AND RETURNS IT, UNTIL IT GETS TO THE END.

Inside the loop, I used the **print** function to show us what the variables num and item contain. I then used an **if** statement to check if the item was an apple or an orange. Based on what the item is, I printed out the action to take.

GETCHILDREN FUNCTION

In the next chapters, we are going to be using one of the built-in functions called GetChildren. Just like our basket of apples and oranges example, the GetChildren will return a table of objects that are contained inside another object. All of the data that makes up your game is stored in what is called the Game object. Think of the Game object as a family. Its "children" objects are what you see in the Explorer window in Roblox Studio. The "children" include the Workspace, Players, Lighting, and other objects. Each "child" or object you see there can also have its own "children." As in most programs, clicking on the arrow next to the object will expand that object, showing you its children. This parent/child relationship can continue multiple times. Although you can only see fifteen or so objects in the Explorer window, those are not the only things inside the Game object. Whhhaaattt!? Yes, there are hidden services that you cannot see, as well as other objects that are not visible.

Let's write a little loop, and see what all we find inside the Game object. Right-click on Workspace, and insert a new script.

```lua
local entireGame = game:GetChildren()

for key, object in pairs(entireGame) do
    print(key, object)
end
```

In this script, we create a **local** variable called `entireGame`. We then call a built-in function on **game** called `GetChildren()`, which returns a list of all the items contained within your game. After that, we run a **for/in** loop and print out the number, and object of everything inside. Go ahead and run this script. You should get about seventy-four objects/items back. That's a big difference compared to the fifteen you actually see in the Explorer window. The `GetChildren()` function is a good approach for keeping track of where you're storing certain objects. For example, say you want a treasure chest in your game to give the player certain items, but further on in your coding you realize you may have forgotten something or changed your mind about what the chest should contain. Using `GetChildren()` will quickly give you a list of what's currently in the chest without you needing to navigate through multiple menus to look for the information you need.

CHAPTER

4

FUNCTIONS

Functions work kind of like loops—they will execute a set of instructions in blocks of code. In this chapter, I'll explain Roblox's different built-in functions and how to create your own functions to perform a task and return a result. Along with functions, we will be discussing triggers, which are specialized events that happen when a certain condition is met. We can use the triggers to connect multiple functions, giving our game world the ability to respond and move. A good custom function can make you smile, but a great custom function can unlock the mysteries of the universe. (No, seriously. You could calculate some string theories and quantum mechanics if you wanted to.)

WHAT IS A FUNCTION?

Functions are instructions for doing specific tasks. These are represented by what are called keywords. You have already worked with the `print` function. When you use a function that is already built into the Lua script, it's called a built-in function. If you create your own function, it is called a custom function. The built-in `print` function takes an argument, then prints it to the console output. We use functions to simplify pieces of code that we would use multiple times throughout the entire code of the game. Here's how to write a function:

```
function name()
    --Code goes here
end
```

Just like variables, you can name a function anything you like. We can add arguments to our functions to be used inside the functions' code. Next, we'll give our function a name, and two parameters, num1 and num2.

```
function add2numbers (num1, num2)
    return num1 + num2
end
```

Now our function is called `add2numbers`. Because of the parameters we set, it knows to take any two numbers we give it, add them together, and return the result. Let's go ahead and enter the following lines after the lines above so we can test our function. Press F5 when you are done to test the results.

```
myResult = add2numbers (5,10)
print(myResult)
```

Output: 15

That's it! You have just written a custom function. This example shows you the general outline of how to write and use functions:

1. Name the function and give it parameters.
2. Write the code so the function performs a task.
3. Call for the function somewhere in the rest of your game's code.

In order to use a function inside your script, the function has to be defined before the first time you use it. Otherwise, the code won't know what to do. If you call add2numbers but have not written what that function does, you will get an error that will halt your script. To see an example of this, take the second part of the code we wrote, and type it above the line where you defined the function ("**function** add2number (num1, num2"). When you run the game, you should get the error "attempt to call global 'add2numbers' (a nil value)." That's telling you that the function doesn't exist.

TRIGGERING EVENTS

A trigger is a command your code will execute when certain things happen. The easiest and most basic trigger is the Touched event. I'll show you how to use that event now. First, in Studio, select the Model tab at the top of your screen. Add a Spawn, and a single Part.

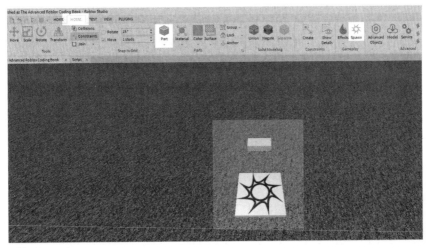

Roblox Corporation

CLICK ON THE MODEL TAB, CLICK SPAWN, THEN CLICK PART.

In the Explorer window on the right, look for the part that you just inserted into the Workspace. Let's rename this part from Part to EventTrigger so that we can identify it from other parts later on if needed.

NAME YOUR PARTS!

IF YOU DO NOT NAME YOUR PARTS WHEN YOU MAKE THEM, YOU WILL SOON FIND YOURSELF IN A WORLD FULL OF OBJECTS NAMED PART WHICH WILL MAKE IT VERY HARD TO FIND SPECIFIC OBJECTS LATER ON. (YES, I HAVE DONE THIS BEFORE.)

WHAT IS AN EVENT?

The next example of code has many ideas that we have already discussed along with one new one. It will have some built-in functions, a custom function, and something new: an Event function. The definition of an Event in a game isn't any different than an event in real life. It's a certain thing that occurs at a specific time.

The Event function we will be working with is Touched and it is inherited from the Part instance. What in the world does that mean? Let me break it down for you.

An Instance is a type of object that has a Parent Class. Instances all have a feature called Inheritance. That means that an instance gets some of its properties and functions from its Parent Class. Part is the Parent Class of a Brick, a Sphere, a Cylinder, and a Wedge. Because they are all subclasses of Part, they will all contain the Touched event as well.

ADDING SCRIPT

Now we need to add a script to our EventTrigger Part. Click on that Part so it has a blue selection box around it. Then right-click on the part, and select Insert Object --> Script. Studio will open up the familiar print("Hello, world!"). Remove that default line and add this code:

```
local myBrick = script.Parent
local function ImTriggered(part)
    print(part)
end

myBrick.Touched:connect(ImTriggered)
```

Notice that before you finished typing `myBrick.`, (don't forget the period!) a dialog box popped up showing you the different properties and events that `myBrick` has. These are the properties, events, and explorer items (other objects) contained in `myBrick`.

- The **blue brick icon** represents a property, like the color, size, name, and position of the brick.
- The **lightning icon** is an indication of an event. We can use these events to run custom functions when one of them triggers (you could also say it "fires").
- The **icon that looks like the Explorer icon** represents items that are inside this object. There should only be one: the script we inserted and are running from.

So, the variable `myBrick` was set by calling **script**.`Parent()`. The script we are running from has the property `Parent`, which is the term for the object the script is sitting in. Using this bit of code allows us to simply type `myBrick` instead of typing out the full path to the EventTrigger Part's location (**game**.`Workspace.EventTrigger`) in order to get information for it. You can still refer to EventTrigger with the long path, but it's just a pain to work with later.

When you have an event fire, you can call the `:connect` built-in function of the event. This will link custom functions that you have created. The function we created is `ImTriggered(part)`. The reason we gave our function the argument Part is because the `.Touched` event passes in the Part that touched it. If you run the game, you should see the baseplate appear in the output window. That's because the Part is touching the baseplate. If you walk over the part, with your avatar you will start to see a bunch of lines in the output of your feet and legs touching the part.

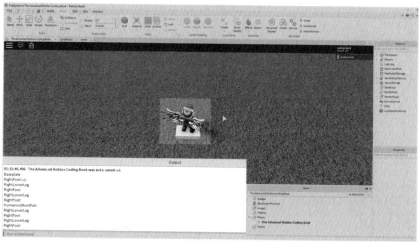

Roblox Corporation

NOW WE CAN TRIGGER OUR FUNCTION ANY TIME SOMETHING TOUCHED THE BRICK!

TAKING THINGS TO THE NEXT LEVEL

But wait. What if we wanted to trigger the function only if a player touched it as opposed to another Part? That means we need to see if the Part that touched our brick belongs to a player. We can do this by taking a look at the Part that was passed in to our function. When a player enters the world, a model of that player's avatar is put into the **game**.Workspace. The avatar has hands, feet, legs, head, torso, and many other objects inside it. One of these items is called Humanoid and it is a special instance that holds information like WalkSpeed, Health, and JumpPower. We need to look and see if the Part that touched us has a parent. If it does, we can search the parent to see if Humanoid is one of its children. Glorious!

Let's change our code to look for this Humanoid. By the way, the Humanoid example has been given many times, by many developers. You are walking in the footsteps of greatness.

```
local myBrick = script.Parent

local function imTriggered(part)
    local humanoid = part.Parent:FindFirstChild("Humanoid")
    if humanoid then
        print("yeah! we found a human!")
    end
end

myBrick.Touched:connect(ImTriggered)
```

When you run your code this time, the baseplate won't show up. The event was still triggered, but we checked the parent of the baseplate, then looked for a child called Humanoid. The game didn't find it, so it never executed the code.

However, if you walk over the Part with a player (that will include the Humanoid child), you will now see that it does detect when the avatar has touched the Part. In fact, it detects it every time an avatar touches the Part. This is not a problem, if we don't mind the code firing whenever a player walks across it.

If we want to only fire it once, we will need to create a custom function called a debounce, which essentially means bounce back. A debounce uses a global variable inside its function. A global variable is a predefined variable that is accessible by all of the scripts throughout your game. The opposite of this is a local variable, which is only accessible by specific parts of script. Local variables are designated with the `local` keyword in the code. It's kinda like the debounce is saying, "Hey, did this run yet? No? Okay, let's run it, but don't let it run again till I'm done. K, thanks."

To add the debounce to our code example, we are going to add a variable to the top of the code called `CanRun`. We are going to set this variable to **true**. Then inside our function, we are going to change our **if** statement so it will check if this variable actually is true. Inside the **if** statement, we will set `CanRun` to **false**, so that it cannot be triggered again until `CanRun` has been set back to **true**. We will add a built-in function called **wait**, and after five seconds, set the `CanRun` back to **true** so we can run over the Part again.

```
local myBrick = script.Parent
local CanRun = true

local function imTriggered(part)
    local humanoid = part.Parent:FindFirstChild("Humanoid")
    if humanoid then
        CanRun = false
        print("yeah! we found a human!")
        wait(5)
        CanRun = true
    end
end

myBrick.Touched:connect(imTriggered)
```

So our entire code contains:

- Built-in functions (**script**, **print**, **wait**)
- A custom function (`ImTriggered`)
- An event trigger (`Touched`)
- A method (`FindFirstChild` and `connect`)

Overall, this example of code contains most of the basic building blocks to most code you will be writing from here on out.

FINISHING UP

The final thing I want to teach you is how to look up all objects and their functions, properties, and events.

1. In Studio, select the View tab at the top.
2. Find and select the Object Browser icon. Don't get overwhelmed by what you see inside here. (I know I did the first time I opened it up!)
3. In the left pane of the window, find Part and click on it. On the right upper pane, you will see a list of everything Part has available to it—every function, every property, and every event. The icons next to the names will show you what each item is:
   1. The light pink block is a function. You call the function with a colon. Like `Part:GetChildren()` and `Part:Get-Mass()`.

2. The blue block is a property. These can be set by using a dot, then the property name, followed by an equal sign. Like this `Part.Name = "NewPart"` and `Part.Parent = `**`game`**`.Workspace`.
3. The yellow lightning icon is an event. These are used with the `connect` method, which can be linked to a custom function, or anonymous function. Like `Part.Touched:connect(MyFunction)`.

In the next chapter, we will start putting all of our knowledge together. If you're feeling overwhelmed, don't worry—the more you use the code, the easier it will be to write.

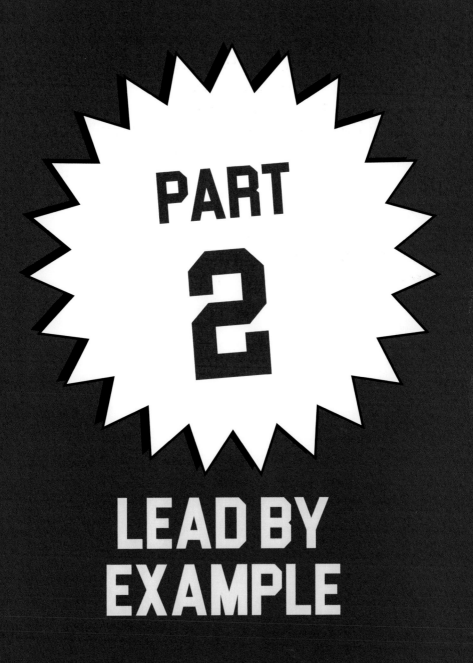

PART 2

LEAD BY EXAMPLE

CHAPTER 5

POWER-UPS AND POWER-DOWNS

Now that we have a basic idea of how to script using common conditions and loops, let's see how we can put these skills to use in games. This chapter is going to concentrate on giving things to the player. This can be anything you can imagine—from something as simple as a sword or health pack—to more sinister and destructive forces, like poison or fire damage. We will also be exploring the different ways to give these things to the player. We'll start by giving the player something when he or she touches an object, then move on to more advanced methods of detection. The limit of what you want to give or do to a player is only limited by your imagination. You're the programmer. Want to turn a player into a bunny because he picked up and ate a carrot? No problem. Want avatars to have the ability to run at lightning speeds? Sure thing. How about letting them have the ability to jump over buildings? Why not?

HUMANOID POWERS

Abilities like running, jumping, and flying live in the Humanoid instance inside the player object. When a player enters a game, there are two items that appear in the Game object:

1. The first is the player themself, and they are located inside the Players menu in the Explorer window with the path: **game**.Players.
2. The second thing that is usually (but not always) created, is the player object. This is the physical representation or avatar of the player. In the Explorer window it appear directly in the Workspace with the path: **game**.Workspace.

The Humanoid instance is located inside the player object directly in the Workspace, not the under the player object inside the Player menu.

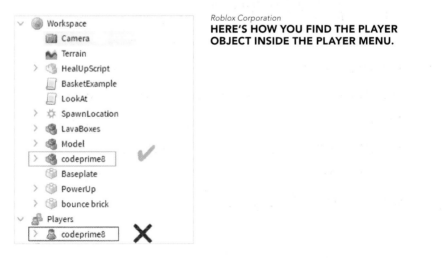

Roblox Corporation

HERE'S HOW YOU FIND THE PLAYER OBJECT INSIDE THE PLAYER MENU.

PROPERTIES OF HUMANOIDS

The Humanoid has the following properties, divided into four groups.

- **Data:** CameraOffset, ClassName, DisplayDistanceType, HealthDisplayDistance, HealthDisplayType, Name, NameDisplayDistance, Parent, RigType, RootPart.
- **Behavior:** Archivable.
- **Control:** AutoJumpEnabled, AutoRotate, FloorMaterial, Jump, MoveDirection, PlatformStand, SeatPart, Sit, TargetPoint, WalkToPart, WalkToPoint.
- **Game:** Health, HipHeight, JumpPower, MaxHealth, MaxSlopeAngle, WalkSpeed.

The main group we will play with now is Game. It's the one that contains the player's health, walk speed, and jumping powers. (Although messing with the other groups is fun too.)

Let's start with some speed-run power-ups, and jump-power power-ups. What are those? Hop in to Studio, and I'll explain everything.

GETTING A PART INTO THE GAME

Before we get into the detailed instructions on how to place and manipulate Parts in a game, let's quickly talk about the Move, Scale, and Rotate tools. They're outlined in *The Ultimate Roblox Book* if you need a refresher.

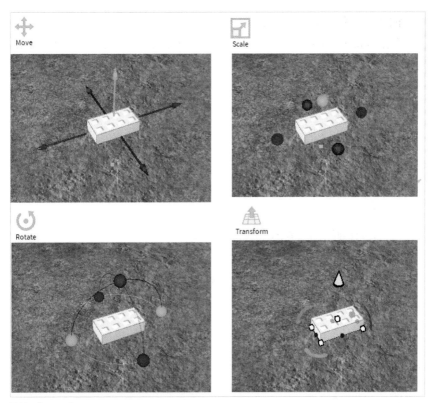

Roblox Corporation
DIFFERENT TOOLS TO BUILD WITH.

Here's a super quick tutorial in the meantime: Any time you use a Move, Rotate, or Scale tool, you will get some colorful adornments attached to the part or model you are working with. The Move tool has arrows, the Scale tool has spheres, and the Rotate tool has rings with spheres. The X-axis is red, the Y-axis is green, and Z-axis is blue. You can modify the default settings for these tools under the Model tab at the top of the screen. The unit of measurement for rotation is represented in degrees. The unit of measurement for movement is studs. There is a fourth tool called Transform. It has a special combination of adornments so you can twist, pivot, and move all at the same time without having to switch between the different tools. While in Transform the small grid in the upper left-hand corner will allow you to move the part relative to another part. Just click on it, then select the part you want to align your part with.

Now that those instructions are out of the way, let's get started placing an object in the game. Let's look at making a coin, as it's one of the simplest objects to make and appears in many, many games. First, add a cylinder into the Workspace. To do this, click on the Model tab at the top of the screen, click on the arrow under Part, and select Cylinder.

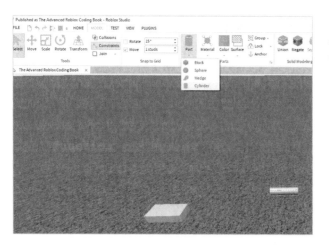

Roblox Corporation
HERE'S HOW TO MAKE A CYLINDER.

Now let's change its size, color, and material. Use the Scale tool, and pull the red balls together. These are your X-axis scale handles. One you have pushed them together, grab the green ball, and move it out four units. Then move the blue ball out four units. Now our coin is starting to look more and more like a coin.

Next, change the color. You can use whatever you like, but I'm going to use green, like "go." Change the color by selecting the Color drop-down menu, and a color palette will appear. Now select a material from the Material drop-down box.

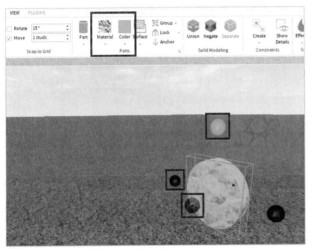

Roblox Corporation
HERE'S HOW TO CHANGE THE COLOR AND MATERIAL OF YOUR PART.

Now we should anchor the part to be sure it doesn't move around during game play. With the part selected, look in the Properties window and scroll down to the Behavior section. Inside this section is how we tell the Part (in this case, our coin) to act when it's in the world. If the Part is not anchored when it comes into the world, it will most likely fall down, get walked over, knocked down, and possibly flung out of the world. Check the box next to Anchored to prevent the Part from moving.

Next, in that same group of Properties, there should be a box labeled CanCollide. By default, this should be on, but we don't want it to be. We are going to have our Part disappear for a while once an avatar runs over it. So uncheck the CanCollide box.

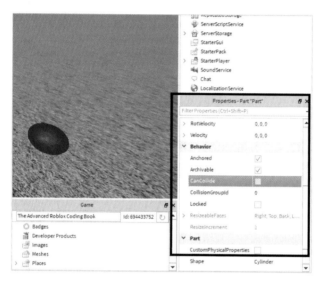

Now we can get to the fun stuff. Right-click on the Part and Insert Object --> Script. We will be working with a server-side script again. First, delete the default `"Hello, world!"` code.

With this script, we will do something a little different. Instead of setting variables at the top of the script, I'm going to add a NumberValue object inside our Part, the cylinder. A Number-Value object will allow us to change the number value in Studio so it will be easier to search for later on.

To add a NumberValue object, right-click on the Part, click Insert Object, then click NumberValue. You should see Value appear under the Part inside the Explorer window. We need to make two more. Right-click on Value, and select Duplicate. Do it again so you have three values in the Part. At this point, change the Part name to PowerUp and the Values to SpeedUpAmount, JumpPowerAmount, and Duration. Rename the script to PowerUpScript.

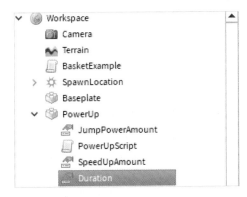

Roblox Corporation
YOU CAN CHANGE THE VALUES WITH THIS SCREEN.

PROGRAMMING A POWER-UP

Now we can start programming our power-up to actually do something. First, let's add some variables at the top that will be defined by the values we added to our Part.

```
local PowerUp = script.Parent
local SpeedUp = PowerUp.SpeedUpAmount.Value
local JumpPower = PowerUp.JumpPowerAmount.Value
local Duration = PowerUp.Duration.Value
local CanTouch = true
```

We have defined PowerUp as the Part, then used PowerUp as the location to look for each one of our values inside the PowerUp Part. (This will allow our script to change based on the values inside the NumberValues instead of us having to open the script to change them.) We will also define a CanTouch so we can debounce later. Let's add our GivePowers function, as you can see in this code:

```
local function GivePowers(part)
    local hum = part.Parent:FindFirstChild("Humanoid")
    if hum and CanTouch then
        CanTouch = false
        local originalWalkSpeed = hum.WalkSpeed
        local originalJumpPower = hum.JumpPower
        hum.WalkSpeed = SpeedUp
        hum.JumpPower = JumpPower
        PowerUp.Transparency = 1.0
        wait(Duration)
        PowerUp.Transparency = 0.0
        hum.WalkSpeed = originalWalkSpeed
        hum.JumpPower = originalJumpPower
        CanTouch = true
    end
end
```

This is the part of the code that will change how fast the player can walk and how high the player can jump for a given number of seconds. It will also make the Part disappear, while the power is in effect. We need to connect a `Touched` event to the function.

```
PowerUp.Touched:Connect(GivePowers)
```

There we go. Now that everything is connected, go to the Part, and change the values to what you would like. The default JumpPower is 50, and the default for WalkSpeed is 16.

I am going to set my Duration to 30, my JumpPowerAmount to 150, and my SpeedUpAmount to 150. This means the player's jump and speed abilities will increase when they touch the `PowerUp` Part. To change the value of the NumberValues, just change the Value field in the Properties window. (Yes, that sentence sounded weird, but it's correct.)

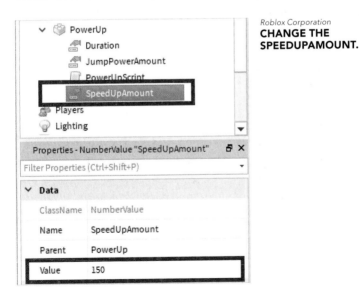

Roblox Corporation
CHANGE THE SPEEDUPAMOUNT.

Now you can press F5 and run your game to test out the new PowerUp Part. You should also try changing the different values around to see what you can do.

DO SOME DAMAGE

Sometimes, you will want to deal damage to a player as part of the game. Maybe a player gets hit by a sword, is hit by a bullet, or falls into lava. No matter which way you choose to do damage, it's done the same way every time: by reducing the Humanoid's health.

SCRIPTING DAMAGE

For this example, I'm going to create a simple lava block that will do damage when an avatar crosses over it.

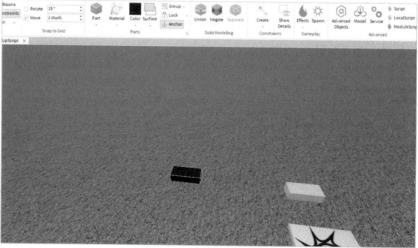

Roblox Corporation
A SIMPLE RED BRICK.

I'm not going to spend a lot of time creating this sample lava block—for your game, you can make it as cool as you want. For now, create a block Part in the world, change its name to LavaBox, anchor it, make it red, and give it some texture. Add a script to the Part, name it LavaBoxScript, and delete the default "Hello, world!".

Just like before, we are going to create some local variables, make a function, and then connect our Touched event to that function. We will go over each part of the script after.

```
local LavaBox = script.Parent
local DamageAmount = 10

local function DealDamage(part)
    local hum = part.Parent:FindFirstChild("Humanoid")
    if hum then
        hum.Health = hum.Health - DamageAmount
    end
end

LavaBox.Touched:Connect(DealDamage)
```

Once it's written, go ahead and run the script to test that you have everything right. You should be able to walk over the brick, see some red flashes from the damage, and eventually your avatar will suffer enough damage that it should oof.

Here's the breakdown of what we did:

1. First, we declared our variables `LavaBox` and `DamageAmount`. The LavaBox is our Part the script is in, so we can reference the part directly using **script**.Parent. Damage-Amount is how much health we are going to take away each time our part is touched.
2. Next, we created our function `DealDamage (part)`, which takes in the Part variable that gets passed to use from the `.Touched` event. We created a local variable inside this function that gets the Part's parent, and then searches for the Humanoid object inside the parent.
3. Our **if** statement checks to see if a variable contains a Humanoid. Then we set the health of the Humanoid's equal to its current health minus our damage amount.
4. The last thing we do is hook up our `.Touched` event to run the `DealDamage` function when it is triggered.

Here are a couple of things to look out for and to consider when programming something like this for an obby, or some other form of damage dealer:

- There is no debounce on this, so the damage will happen on every touch.
- The player will receive 10 damage each time, so to inflict 100 damage, the event will need to trigger ten times. If you would like the avatar to oof instantly, just set the damage to 100, or even more.

By using the `MaxHealth`, we can insure that the player will oof no matter what their current health is.

```
hum.Health = hum.Health - hum.MaxHealth
```

Now here is the next kicker. What if you have 20, or 50, or 1,000 of these Parts in your game? You would have to add a script to each one of them, and that would take up a lot of processing power on the server. I don't know about you, but I really don't want that many scripts running in the background waiting for someone to hit the one brick. Let's try and fix that by using only one script to find all the LavaBoxes in the game, and connect them to the same function. This way any time one of the boxes is touched, the same action is performed no matter how many boxes we have.

1. In the Explorer window, move the script out of the Lava-Box, and place it into ServerScriptService. You can move the script by just dragging it with the mouse, or by right-clicking on it, using cut, then right-clicking on Server-ScriptService, and selecting paste into.
2. Now that our script is no longer in the Part, we will not be able to use the **script**.Parent function to get the part. Also, because we are going to be dealing with multiple parts, we are going to have to get them all.
3. Go back into the Workspace, and select your LavaBox. Press CTRL + D or CMD + D to duplicate the part, then move them around or in patterns so you have a bunch of them.

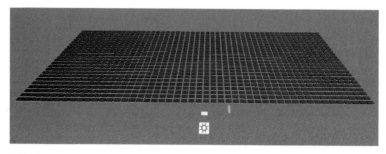

Roblox Corporation
NOW WE HAVE LOTS OF LAVABOXES.

4. Inside our script we are going to delete the LavaBox variable, and change the Touched event. Replace the `LavaBox.Touched:Connect(DealDamage)` with the following code:

```
for k,n in pairs(game.Workspace:GetChildren()) do
    if n.Name == "LavaBox" then
        n.Touched:Connect(DealDamage)
    end
end
```

5. We used a for loop to go through all the children in the Workspace. Then every time we find a Part named LavaBox, we connect its `Touched` function to the `Deal-Damage` function. Press F5 and test out our new script. No matter what LavaBlock you run over, the same effect should occur. This is a great idea for an obby that has many damage blocks, without using up a lot of script threads.

LIFE GIVER

If we deal damage by taking away health from a user, then it makes sense that we can heal them by adding health. By default, users will regain health lost at a rate of one hit point per second. In this example, we are going to create an item that looks like a green plus symbol. (Feel free to make yours look however you like.) I will make mine look like this:

Roblox Corporation
MY SAMPLE HEALUP ITEM.

I will quickly go over how I created the Part, if you would like to make one for yourself.

1. Create a Part by selecting Part from the Model menu
2. Change Size to 3,1,1 in the properties
3. Set Anchored to true
4. Set CanCollide to false
5. Change Color to green (#00ff00)
6. Change Material to Glass

7. Change Transparency to 0.25
8. Select Part and press CTRL + D to duplicate the part
9. Change the new Part's rotation to 0,0,90 (you may have to unanchor it)
10. Select both Parts by holding SHIFT and clicking on the first part
11. Click Union from the Model menu, or press CTRL + SHIFT + G
12. Move the Part up so it's about chest height (about 2 studs off the ground)
13. Change Orientation to 0,0,0
14. Right-click on the Unioned Part, and Insert Object -> Particle Emitter
15. Select the Particle Emitter from the Explorer window
16. Change LifeTime to 1, 5
17. Change RotSpeed to 100
18. Change Color to green (#00ff00)
19. Change Acceleration to 0, 1, 0
20. Change Transparency to 0.7

Great! I know there were a lot of steps in building that, but it's for a reason. You just practiced moving around the various Studio windows, changing different properties, and seeing all the different types of values you can use! Even making something as simple as a power-up can become time-consuming and you haven't even coded it to do something yet. Practicing how to build will make you appreciate the work developers put into their games.

I hope this little power-up has given you insight to what it takes to build before the code.

Now let's get to scripting. Rename your Unioned Part to HealUp, then add a script to it. Rename the script to HealUp-Script and delete the `Hello, world!`. Here comes something new. Add a second script. Rename this one to Animate. That's right: We are going to make it spin. Inside the Animate script type out the following code.

```
local Healer = script.Parent
local start_pos = Healer.Position
local start_ori = Healer.Orientation

Healer.Anchored = true
Healer.CanCollide = false

while(1) do
    for x = 0,180,5 do
        wait()
        Healer.Position = start_pos
        Healer.Orientation = Vector3.new(0,x,0)
    end
end
```

Here's what this code does:

1. We created our local variable for our object, `Healer`, then stored its starting position and its starting orientation into our `start_pos`, `start_ori` variables.
2. We set the Part Anchored property to true, and CanCollide property to false.

3. Next, we created an infinite loop. (Wait! I thought you said those are bad? I never said they were bad, but I did say to watch out for them.) See that `wait()` statement inside the **for** loop? If that was not there, the whole server would stop while it waited for this code to end. So, repeating the animations of an item within a game are a good use of an infinite loop.

4. Next up, we created a **for** loop to go from 1 to 180. Now if our object was not the same on front and back, or side to side, then we would have gone to 360. In our case the front and the back look the same, so we only need to rotate it half a circle. The last number is to count by 5s or move 5 degrees. Then on each pass of the **for** loop, we set the location back to the same position it had at the beginning. With each pass we set the rotation to whatever x is. This means that on each iteration, the plus is going to look like it's spinning. You can play with the variables to see what it does. If you want it to spin slower, you can change the wait to have a time, or change the steps from 5 to 1.

IMPROVING HEALTH

Next, we need our HealUp to actually do its job. Let's program it. You should start to see how all the scripts are similar.

```
local Healer = script.Parent
local HealAmount,TimeBetweenHeals = 10,5
```

```
function HealMe(part)
    local hum = part.Parent:FindFirstChild("Humanoid")
    if hum and Healer.Transparency ~= 1.0 then
        hum.Health = hum.Health + HealAmount
        local original_trans = Healer.Transparency
        Healer.Transparency = 1.0
        Healer.ParticleEmitter.Enabled = false
        wait(TimeBetweenHeals)
        Healer.Transparency = original_trans
        Healer.ParticleEmitter.Enabled = true
    end
end
Healer.Touched:Connect(HealMe)
```

See how similar it is? Variables at the top, functions in the middle, connect them at the end. This time I did something a little different for our `HealAmount`, and `TimeBetweenHeals` variables. I declared both of them at the same time on the left side of the "=" symbol, and assigned values to them both on the right. Although you can declare and assign different types of variables, I recommend that you keep strings and numbers separated. You don't *have* to, but I think it makes it cleaner.

For the `HealMe` function, we follow the same steps as before:

1. Check the Part that touched us for a Humanoid inside its parent.
2. Check our Part's transparency. That's because our transparency is going to become our debounce, so we don't need an actual debounce variable. If the part is already invisible, don't let the user step on it again.

3. Once we have verification that we can, give the user the Health amount we assigned in our `HealAmount` variable.

4. Get the current transparency of our Part and store it for later, then set our transparency to 1.0 so it cannot be seen in the world.

5. Turn off the particles. Otherwise it will look like the particles are still flowing out from nothing. We can turn them off by setting our Enabled property to false. Nice!

6. All that's left is to create a "time out" for the Part, meaning it won't appear for a certain amount of time. We use our `TimeBetweenHeals` variable in a **wait** statement. Once our **wait** function is complete, we reassign the transparency and position, then enable the particles again.

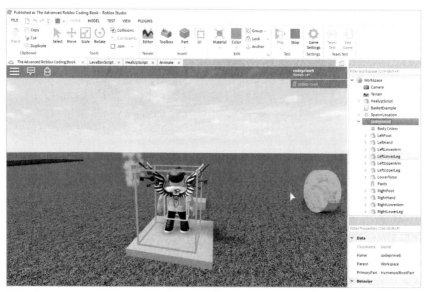

Roblox Corporation
FIND YOUR HUMANOID'S PROPERTIES.

Now, to test this out, we are going to have to deal some damage to our avatar. Go ahead and run the game by pressing F5. When the game starts, find your avatar in the Explorer window. When you select your avatar, you will see a blue box appear around it. Expand out your avatar object, and find the Humanoid inside. When you click on Humanoid, you can now change its properties.

Find Health under the Game menu in the Properties window, and change it to 50. This will deal some damage to your avatar. Now you can click on the Workspace and move your avatar over to the HealUp object. Watch your life when you walk through the object.

Roblox Corporation
YOU CAN SEE THE ANIMATION WHEN YOU WALK THROUGH THE OBJECT.

FINISHING UP

In this chapter, we have learned how to give out some simple powers, deal some damage, and heal our players. There is so much more that can be done, but we are just touching the fundamentals of how to make things happen. (I mean, we haven't even given out weapons yet!) I hope you have played around with the scripts, and experimented a little bit with changing things to your liking. You have the tools to change Part properties, detect the Humanoid, and trigger events based on what you find. Use my code examples, play with them, and make them your own.

CHAPTER

6

BEAM ME UP

Making characters run and jump is definitely fun, but transporting them to other spots in your game really kicks things up a notch. In this chapter, you'll learn how to move players from one point to another using scripts.

TELEPORTATION

There will come a time when you want to move a player from one place to another in your game world using teleportation pads. If you try to just move the or avatar's head, or torso, you will get a mess. Moving a Part will detach it from the avatar, and you will have an oof.

Roblox Corporation
THAT'S NOT WHAT WE WANTED TO HAPPEN.

SETUP

Let's start by setting up our teleportation pads. Now, you can use anything you want as a teleportation pad: a door, floor, item, NPC. It doesn't really matter, but for the purpose of this example we are going to stick with just two simple Parts. In the Workspace, add a Part, and name it Teleport1A.

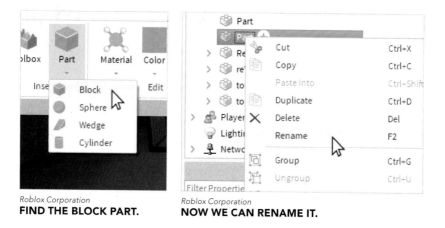

Roblox Corporation
FIND THE BLOCK PART.

Roblox Corporation
NOW WE CAN RENAME IT.

Roblox Corporation
HERE'S WHAT IT LOOKS LIKE WHEN WE RENAME IT.

You can change the look of the part if you want. I'll choose blue, squarish, and foil for the material. With the Part selected, press CTRL + D to duplicate the part.

Roblox Corporation
HERE'S OUR ONE BLUE BLOCK.

Roblox Corporation
NOW IT'S TWICE AS TALL.

Change the name of this second Part to Teleport1B and change its color to something other than blue. I will go with pink.

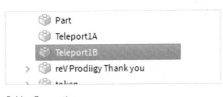

Roblox Corporation
NOW WE'VE NAMED THE SECOND PART.

Roblox Corporation
THE SECOND BLOCK IS PINK NOW.

In the Explorer window, drag Teleport1B into Teleport1A so that it becomes a child of the first Teleport. This will make things easier to find later in the Lua script.

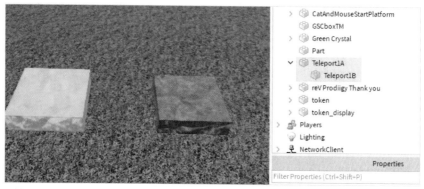

LET'S PUT TELEPORT1B INSIDE TELEPORT1A.

Be sure that you anchor your Parts so they don't go flying off when you run over them. As a reminder, to anchor a Part, select the Part, then go to the Properties window, and check the Anchored property.

CHECK THE ANCHORED BOX TO KEEP THE PARTS TOGETHER.

Properties - Part "Part"	
Filter Properties (Ctrl+Shift+P)	
> RotVelocity	0, 0, 0
> Velocity	0, 0, 0
∨ **Behavior**	
Anchored	☑
Archivable	☑
CanCollide	☑
CollisionGroupId	0
Locked	☐
> ResizeableFaces	Right, Top, Back, Left, Bottom, Front
ResizeIncrement	1

Now we are going to add a Server script to the Teleport1A and get things moving. Click the ⊕ symbol on the side of Teleport1A.

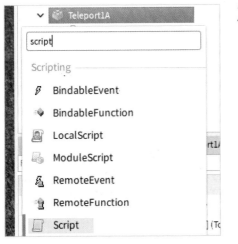

CLICK ON THE PLUS SYMBOL TO ADD A SCRIPT.

Type out the word *script* in the search box. Be sure you click on Script, and not LocalScript.

ADDING A SCRIPT.

THE CODE

Now we can get into the code. For consistency's sake, go ahead and rename the script to TeleportScript. This will help you identify what the script does later on. Delete the **print** ("Hello, world!").

There are many ways we could make this script. For now, we will make the two pads teleport between each other. This way all you will have to do is move the two pads to the teleportation points you want in the world. We will set up our reference variables first, so we can easily get their properties.

```
local Teleport1A = script.Parent
local Teleport1B = script.Parent.Teleport1B
```

We will need to create a Time Out variable that will trigger if someone goes through the teleportation location, so they don't instantly teleport again once they hit the other side.

```
local canTeleport = true
```

We will need to create two functions—one for each of the pads that will be doing the teleporting. The reason for this is because the Touched function does not tell us which part was touched, only the person or Part that touched it. These functions do not do anything for now.

```
function TeleportA(part)
end

function TeleportB(part)
end
```

Let's connect our two pads to the functions so they trigger when someone (or something) touches them.

```
Teleport1A.Touched:connect(TeleportA)
Teleport1B.Touched:connect(TeleportB)
```

Our pads' Touched functions are now linked. It's time to make them do some teleporting. Here is the code. I will break it down in sections:

```
function TeleportA(part)
    local hum = part.Parent:FindFirstChild
    ("HumanoidRootPart")
    if hum then
        if canTeleport then
            canTeleport = false
            hum.CFrame = Teleport1B.CFrame + Vector3.
            new(0,5,0)
            wait(5)
            canTeleport = true
        end
    end
end

function TeleportB(part)
    local hum = part.Parent:FindFirstChild
    ("HumanoidRootPart")
    if hum then
        if canTeleport then
            canTeleport = false
            hum.CFrame = Teleport1A.CFrame + Vector3.
            new(0,5,0)
            wait(5)
            canTeleport = true
        end
    end
end
```

Both functions are the same, except for which Teleport `CFrame` we are going to use (I'll explain the CFrame in a moment). In the first line, we get the parent of the Part that made contact with our pad, then look to see if there is a `HumanoidRootPart` inside that object.

```
local hum = part.Parent:FindFirstChild("HumanoidRootPart")
if hum then
```

If the Part was Humanoid, we check to make sure we are allowed to teleport them.

```
if canTeleport then
```

As long as everything has checked out, we will set `canTeleport` to **false**, and teleport the user.

```
canTeleport = false
hum.CFrame = Teleport1A.CFrame + Vector3.new(0,5,0)
wait(5)
canTeleport = true
```

The `HumanoidRootPart` is what we want to move. The CFrame contains the position, rotation, and direction that an avatar or Part has. We set the user's CFrame to the CFrame of our `Teleport1A`, and make sure it's five units above the Part. Otherwise, your avatar would be stuck in the middle of the teleportation pad. After the teleport has been performed, we wait for five seconds, then set our `canTeleport` variable back to **true**.

Now it's time to test. Start your game by pressing F5 or selecting Play from the Test tab at the top of the screen.

Run over either one of the pads, and you should end up on the opposite pad.

Roblox Corporation
BEFORE TELEPORTATION, THE AVATAR IS WALKING NEAR THE BLUE BLOCK.

Roblox Corporation
AFTER TELEPORTATION, THE AVATAR IS SUDDENLY ON THE PINK BLOCK.

As I said before, there are many ways you could teleport players to different areas. The main point is to use the `HumanoidRootPart` CFrame and not the torso, head, or some other piece of it.

THE CFRAME

When we teleported our avatar, we used the CFrame, but I didn't explain what a CFrame is. A CFrame is essentially an invisible frame around an object that designates the object's position and orientation in 3D space. Before we get too far into the CFrame, let me explain what a `Vector3` is. A vector consists of three numbers: X, Y, and Z. These three numbers represent a point in space—in our case, a point in the Workspace.

Now, a vector doesn't have to just represent a point in space. It can also represent a color like red, green, or blue, or it could represent a rotation, such as yaw, pitch, or roll. Anytime you need three numbers to represent something, you can use a `Vector3`.

CFrame uses `Vector3` in some different ways. The one that we have already used is the position `CFrame.new(Vector3)`. You may have noticed that when we teleported our avatar, we were no longer facing the same way as when we stepped on the platform. That's because we just took the CFrame of the teleport pad we were going to, and used its CFrame for our avatar, rather than giving the avatar its own CFrame.

HOW TO CREATE A CFRAME

To get a better understanding of CFrame, let's go over the different ways to create one. To just create a CFrame with no properties, you can use `CFrame.new()`. But there are a bunch of "constructors" that allow you to set properties of a CFrame. (Find the full list on http://robloxdev.com/api-referencedatatype/CFrame.)

- `CFrame.new(Vector3 pos)`—Takes in a `Vector3` as the position of the CFrame.
- `CFrame.new(Vector3 pos, Vector3 lookAt)`—Uses the first for a position, then the second as a position to look at. It sets the forward position to point in the direction of the second vector.

- `CFrame.new(number x, number y, number z)`—A CFrame with just an X, Y, Z position.
- `CFrame.new(number x, number y, number z, number qx, number qy, number qz, number qw)`—Yes, this one is complicated. The first three (x,y,z) are the position, and the last four (qx,qy,qz,qw) are its rotation in quaternion form.

For now we are not going to get into Euler rotations, or quaternion calculations. We could write an entire new book about those (and people have). Let's just stick with some simple position and `lookAt` vectors.

In the Workspace, add a script. Type out the following code with the exception of "`codeprime8`"—type the name of your avatar instead of mine.

```
local myPart = Instance.new("Part",workspace)
local myPos = Vector3.new(0,10,0)
local myLook = Vector3.new(0,1,0)
local myCFrame = CFrame.new(myPos,myLook)
myPart.Anchored = true

while (1) do
    myPart.CFrame = myCFrame
    codeprime8 = workspace:WaitForChild("codeprime8")
    myLook = codeprime8.HumanoidRootPart.Position
    myCFrame = CFrame.new(myPos,myLook)
    wait()
end
```

Here's a breakdown of the code:

- For the first variable `myPart`, we create a new Part, and set its parent to the Workspace.
- For the second variable we create a position vector. This is where we want our Part to appear.
- The `myLook` is a vector to have our "forward" to point. We only use this once to create the CFrame.
- The next variable is `myCFrame`, and uses the first two variables for the position and `lookAt` arguments.
- We then set the `myParts` anchored to **true**. This will prevent it from trying to fall and follow physics.
- We create a **while** loop. Yes, it's another infinite loop, so be sure you put your **wait()** statement in there somewhere. On the first iteration of this loop, we set our Part's CFrame to the `myCFrame`.
- Next we create a variable to look for our avatar. We use **game**.Workspace:WaitForChild("codeprime8") so the script will wait until our avatar has appeared in the game. When it does, our variable will now be set to our avatar.
- We then set our `myLook` variable to be equal to our avatar's `HumanoidRootPart` position. Basically, wherever our avatar is, that's what we want for our `lookAt` vector.
- We then rebuild our CFrame with the new positions.

Now try running the game and watch as the creepy Part follows your avatar around no matter where you move.

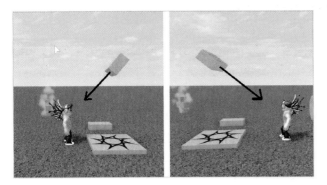

THE BLOCK NOW SEEMS LIKE IT'S LOOKING AT THE AVATAR.

MORE ADVANCED CFRAME WORK

Going further with this, we can now make it a little more complicated. We are going to search for all the players in the game, get their positions, find the one that is closest to us, and use them as our lookAt. Sound hard? Not when we break it down. All we need to do is create a new function.

Type out the following just above our loop and we will go over it after you are done. Note: some lines are wider than this book will allow. If you see a _ in the code, the next line is a continuation of the line you are on. Do not type the _. Just keep typing on the current line.

```
local function getClosestAvatarPosition(part)
    local Players = game.Players:GetChildren()
    local PlayerPositions = {}
```

```
if #PlayerPositions then

    for key, Player in pairs(Players) do
        local plName = Player.Name
        local plPos = game.Workspace:WaitForChild
        (Player.Name).HumanoidRootPart.Position
        local plDis = (part.Position - plPos).
        magnitude
        table.insert(PlayerPositions,key,{plName,
        plPos,plDis})
    end

    Hunting = PlayerPositions[1]

    for x = 1,#PlayerPositions,1 do
        if PlayerPositions[x][3] < Hunting[3]then
            Hunting = PlayerPositions[x]
        end
    end
    if Hunting then
        return Hunting[2]
    else
        return part.Position
    end

else
    return part.Position
end
end
```

You will also need to modify the loop. Here is the what the code looks like.

```
while (1) do
    myPart.CFrame = myCFrame
    myLook = getClosestAvatarPosition(myPart)
    myCFrame = CFrame.new(myPos,myLook)
    wait()
end
```

Whew! That's some typing right there. You may have noticed that this code has a lot of different parts. I know there are many ways it could be written, and I will not claim that mine is the best way, but I know it works.

- To break it down, look at what we are doing in the loop. We are setting the `myLook` value by calling the `getCloset-AvatarPosition(myPart)` function. In this function we could pass in any part, and find the position of the avatar closest to it. Inside the function we set a couple of variables:
  - `Players` is set to a table of all players currently in the game.
  - `PlayerPositions` is created as an empty table. We are going to use this in just a second.
- Our first `if` statement uses `#Players` which is equal to the number of players in the game. If there are no players that number would be 0, or `false`. In the case of no players, we just return the Part's position.
- In the first `for` loop, we go through each player found. On each iteration of this loop we set three variables `plName`, `plPos`, and `plDis`, which are the Name, Position, and Distance from our Part's position. You want to make

sure you are using a `WaitForChild` function to find the player object, because there could be a player that just joined the game, but whose avatar has not appeared yet.

- We get the distance between the player and the Part by taking the Part position minus the player position. The function `.magnitude` is a built-in function for calculating distance, or absolute numbers.
- We store our values into the `PlayerPositions` table by calling **table.insert**.
  - The first variable is the table we want to save our data to.
  - The second is the position to insert it. In this case, we just use the same position as the avatars.
  - And the last variable is the actual data to insert. In our case we want to save three things, so we place them in brackets {}.

The table itself now looks something like this.

1	codeprime8	{3,1,8}	5.22223
2	Player1	{2,1,9}	6.63333

In order to reference tables within tables, you have to use identifiers after the variable names. So `PlayerPositions` is a reference to the table itself. `PlayerPositions[1]` is a reference to the first table. And `PlayerPositions[1][1]` is the string value "codeprime8". Hang in there. I just saw the look on your face.

I promise it's not as hard as it sounds. Just think of it kind of like street addresses. If you say "who lives in USA," I wouldn't know what you're talking about. Same with "who lives in Missouri, USA"—I'm still confused. "Springfield, Missouri, USA" is closer, but still not specific enough. "PO Box 8004, Springfield, Missouri, USA." AH! That's much better. The `codeprime8` is like the exact address. Onward.

After we have built the table of usernames, positions, and distances, we need to find out which one is the smallest. To do this, we are going to need to loop through the table again, and check distance. We set a new variable called `Hunting`, and make it equal to the first distance found in our table at `Player Position[1][3]`. Using a **for** loop, we go from one to the number of PlayerPositions in our table. We check each player position by referencing `PlayerPositions[x][3]` and seeing if it is less than our current `Hunting` positions distance [3], then we set our new `Hunting` position to the current `PlayerPositions[x]`.

After we have run through the entire table and got the smallest distance between the Part and our avatar, we check to see if the position is valid. If it is good, return the position (`Hunting[2]`). If it's not a valid position, then return the Part's position to prevent errors. To test out our code you can run a local server by going to the Test tab at the top of the screen, making sure Local Server, and 2 Players is selected from the drop-downs, and pressing Start.

Roblox Corporation

TEST YOUR CODE WITH THESE MENU DROP-DOWNS.

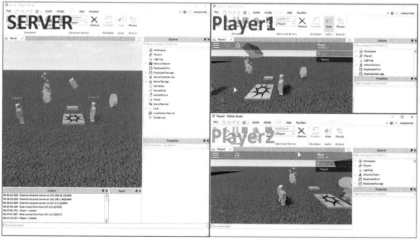

Roblox Corporation

WITH THIS SCREEN, YOU CAN SEE WHAT WILL HAPPEN WHEN YOU RUN YOUR SCRIPT.

You should get three new windows. The first one is just like the Studio window that is already open. It acts as the server so you can see what is happening. The second and third window will be Player Client windows, and you will be able to control Player1 and Player2. When you are testing to see if a script will work correctly once published, you should test it in the local server first. If it doesn't work here, it will not work on the published version.

Now, move your players around. You will see our block will point at the player that is closest to our part. This technique can be very useful if making something like a Turret Gun that would aim at players, or cat's eyes that watch them as they pass by. You could also set some sort of minimal distance for an interaction. That way if a player is not within a certain range, the script will just ignore them.

What's great about this example is that you not only get used to the `Position` and `LookAt` vectors in a CFrame, but you also used the Search function to get other objects, set them into a table, search on those objects we found, and determine an outcome. Good job!

BODY MOVERS

Now that we have messed around a little bit with making Parts look at things, how about getting a Pet to follow us around? Here I am going to introduce something called Body Movers. These are like little engines that will move around physical Parts in the Workspace. The main one we are going to work with to build our pet is BodyPosition.

In this example, I have a mesh, or basic shape, that I created for my Theus game. You may download it for free from here www.roblox.com/library/1257304279/Meshes-ship2-2.

Meshes/ship2 (2)

By codeprime8 ⬤ Item Owned

This item is available in your inventory.

Price   Free

Type   MeshPart

Genres   All

Updated   Aug. 06, 2018

Description   Its a ship! :D

Roblox Corporation
**HERE'S THE
MESH I MADE.**

You can also add the mesh in Studio by clicking on the View tab at the top of the screen, clicking Toolbox, changing, the search to Meshes, and typing in "Meshes-ship2-2." The first one should look like the ship. (Oh, side note. It's HUGE! I made it with Blender 3D, and creating meshes is outside the scope of this chapter. Will cover some more in Part 3.)

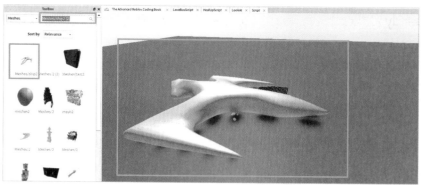

Roblox Corporation
CHANGING THE PROPERTIES OF THE MESH.

Once you have added the mesh Part to the Workspace, go ahead and scale it WAY down. I recommend clicking on the Properties window and setting the size to 4,1,5. This will make it much smaller and more manageable.

Next we are going to need the texture I created for the ship. I have also made this free, and please forgive the artistry. Go to the TextureID property of our new mesh, and type in the number 1257302541. When you press Enter, the texture will change from gray to the one I have provided.

Roblox Corporation
THE PROCESS OF CHANGING THE TEXTURE AND COLOR OF THE MESH.

Okay! Now that we have our mesh part all set up, we are ready to get it moving around and hanging out with us. (By the way, you can use whatever meshes you like. You don't have to stick with a ship. Just make sure you know which way the X-axis is facing. It will be important.)

Right-click on your mesh in the Explorer window and add in a script. Rename the script to PetScript. We will still be working with server-side script. Inside the script, we are going to create the BodyPosition body mover. We'll look for our avatar, then make our ship look at us, and finally, when we move, we are going to have our ship move that way as well. We are also going to put a little bit of a buffer on it, so that it will not be in the exact same position as our avatar. Let's type out the script.

```
local NewPet = script.Parent

NewPet.CanCollide = false

local PetPos = Instance.new("BodyPosition", NewPet)
local PetGyro = Instance.new("BodyGyro", NewPet)
PetGyro.MaxTorque = Vector3.new(400000,400000,400000)
local Owner = 'codeprime8'

while(1) do
    wait()
    local OwnerObj = workspace:WaitForChild(Owner)
    local OwnerPos = OwnerObj.HumanoidRootPart.Position
    local StopAt = ((OwnerPos - NewPet.Position).
    magnitude - 5) * 1000
    PetPos.P = StopAt
    PetPos.Position = OwnerPos + Vector3.new(0,10,0)
    PetGyro.CFrame = OwnerObj.HumanoidRootPart.CFrame
end
```

Let's run through the code:

1. The first thing we did was set NewPet to **script.**parent.
2. Next we made sure that our pet is not going to bump into things by turning CanCollide off.
3. In order for us to make our pet move and look around, we need two body movers:

1. With `PetPos`, we created a new `BodyPosition` instance and place it into our pet.

2. With `PetGyro` we create a `BodyGyro` and place it into our pet as well. The `PetPos` we don't have to mess with much, but with the `PetGyro`, we are going to have to set its MaxTorque. When you create a Gyro, the default MaxTorque is 400000, 0, 400000. That means there is no gyro on the Y-axis. We don't want that. We want our pet to be able to move to the same rotation as our avatar.

4. The next thing we do is set an owner. This will be the avatar model we look for in the Workspace. Now we can get things moving.

5. I then created a **while** loop with a **wait()** function inside, because that's what we have been working with so far. We created a local `OwnerObj` variable to look for and hold our avatar's object. Once it's found, we set a new local variable, `OwnerPos`, to get the `HumanoidRootPart`'s position.

6. Now we have to use a little math to determine where we want our pet to stop. To do this, I have taken the owner's position minus the pet's position and got the Magnitude. This is how far away the pet is from the owner. I then used minus five because I would like the pet to stop pursuing us about five studs away. I then take that number and multiply it by 1,000. If we don't, then the part would slowly fall below the baseplate, and look funny doing so. (I know, I tried it.)

7. Now we give the `StopAt` variable to `PetPos.P`, which basically is the amount of Power our Part is going to use to get to its target position. Low power means it's not going to be very aggressive. High power means it's going to try to get there as fast as possible.

8. Next we wed the `PetPos.Position` to our owner. I don't want the pet to be inside the owner, so I added ten studs to the Y position by adding a new **Vector3** value: 0, 10, 0. We then set the `PetGyro.CFrame` to the owner's CFrame. The cool thing about the `BodyPosition` and the `BodyGyro` is that they are just like CFrames, except they ignore the parts that they don't use. `BodyPosition` doesn't care about the rotation, and `BodyGyro` doesn't care about the position. So we just set `PetGryo` to our owner's CFrame, and we are done.

Now the pet will look in the same direction as our owner. Take your pet out for a spin by pressing F5 and running the game.

Roblox Corporation
THE MESH "PET" WILL FOLLOW THE AVATAR AROUND.

FINISHING UP

In this chapter, we have moved around our avatars, messed around with CFrames, and added some body movers to make a space pet. There is so much more that you can be do with scripts to move Parts around. We have barely scratched the surface.

To give you a few more ideas about what you can do with Body Movers, try making a Part that will only move around on its X- and Z-axis. That way your avatar could bump it around, but it would never go up or down. Here are some other ideas:

- Hoverboards (like the ones from *Back to the Future*, not the ones with the wheels).
- Homing missiles! Those would be cool.
- Swarming bees.
- Clouds that drift around in the sky.
- Platforms that move from one point to another.

Okay, okay, you get the picture. Let's end the chapter. BOOP!

CHAPTER 7

THE DATA KEEPER

There are a lot of reasons why you would want to save information in your games. Maybe you want the game to remember what level a player is on, how much gold they have, or what's in their backpack. You may also want to save details about the environment itself, like how many servers are currently running, or how many times a certain item in the game has been collected. We can also ask the question, "Does your game need to save anything?" Sometimes that is a very vital question. If there is no reason to save anything, then why use it? This chapter is going to cover how to save both individual data for the player and environmental data about the server. We will go over the time-honored leaderboard, as well as the DataStoreService class.

THE LEADERBOARD

If you have played games like Lumber Tycoon 2, Jail Break, or Farming Simulator, then you should be pretty familiar with what a leaderboard is. It usually appears at the top right side of the screen and displays information about the players that are in the game, like money, level, experience points, and what team each player is on.

codeprime8 Account: 13+	Money 15,738,496
codeprime8	15,738,496
talon6442	32
bumbumbabapopo	20
metrowinner5783	20

Roblox Corporation

THE LEADERBOARD APPEARS IN THE UPPER RIGHT-HAND CORNER.

Before we can start using the DataStoreService to save stuff, we are going to need to enable the API service on our game. API stands for application program interface. It allows your game to interact with a Roblox server. It includes a feature called Data

Stores. Using this feature is how we're able to check the save data of any user, like what level they are, so when they leave and log back in to the game, all of their save data is still there. To do this, you will need to open the Roblox website. Go to the Create link at the top. Find the game that you want to enable saving on. Click on the Settings button (which looks like a little gear icon), and select Configure Game.

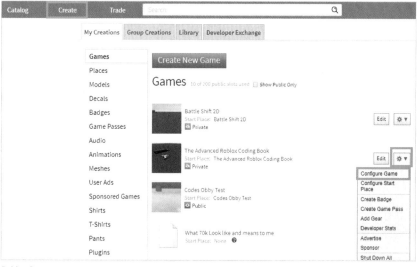

Roblox Corporation
SELECT THESE BUTTONS TO CONFIGURE YOUR GAME.

In the Basic Settings menu of Configure Game, check the box that says Enable Studio Access to API Services. Once you have it checked, click Save, and you are now ready to use some DataStores.

Configure Game

Basic Settings	**Basic Settings**
Avatar Settings	Name:
Places	The Advanced Roblox Coding Book
Created Places	Privacy:
Developer Products	○ Public ❓
	● Private ❓

Enable Studio Access to API Services: ☑

Save   Cancel

Roblox Corporation
HERE'S HOW TO ACCESS THE API SERVICES.

Although a leaderboard is not necessary for saving data, it's something you should use to let the players know where they rank amongst the others playing.

Let's create a simple board to show money, like in Lumber Tycoon 2. Add a script to the ServerScriptService, and name it LeaderBoardScript.

Roblox Corporation
LET'S NAME THE SCRIPT SERVERSCRIPTSERVICE.

Now open up the script and type in the following code:

```
local function AddBoard2Player(player)
    local board = Instance.new("Model",player)
    board.Name = "leaderstats"

    local money = Instance.new("IntValue",board)
    money.Name = "Money"
    money.Value = 0
end

game.Players.PlayerAdded:Connect(AddBoard2Player)
```

This script is very straightforward.

1. We created a function AddBoard2Player and it takes one argument: the player.
2. Inside the function, we create a variable called board with a new Model instance. We set the parent as the player. Note, this is the player in the Game object. Not the players listed within the Workspace.
3. Then we set the name of our board variable to leader-stats. This is vital because if the model is not named leaderstats, then nothing will show up.
4. Once we have the leaderstats model, we can now create values to put in there. Let's add a money variable. We make the money variable by creating a new instance of IntValue and setting its parent as the board. Now, even though our variable is named Money, that is not the object's name. We have to set the Name property

so it shows up on the board. We set the `.Name` value to "`Money`" and the value to 0. Last, we connect the function to the `game.Players.PlayerAdded` event. This way, every time a player is added, a new board is created and added to all of the players.

To test this out, we need to run the script and change the values. You can do this in a script, or by adding some parts into the world that will add money. What I am going to do is add a sphere Part, change its material to neon yellow, name it MoneyGlob in the Explorer window, and give it a script that will increase money by five when stepped on, then destroy the glob.

Roblox Corporation
HERE'S OUR MONEYGLOB PART.

When you add the script, name it MoneyGiver, and type out the following code:

```lua
local me = script.Parent

local function GiveMoney(part)
    local hum = part.Parent:FindFirstChild("Humanoid")
    local plName = part.Parent.Name

    if hum then
        local player = game.Players:FindFirstChild(plName)
        local money = player.leaderstats["Money"]
        money.Value = money.Value + 5
        me:Destroy()
    end
end

me.Touched:Connect(GiveMoney)
```

Now this script is mostly like the other scripts we have written up to this point. I'll go through it quickly:

1. We set the variable me to the script's parent, MoneyGlob Part.
2. Then we created a GiveMoney function that takes in the Part.
3. We checked to see if that Part belongs to a player. We set the variable plName to the parent's name to use later. If it is a player, we would create a variable called player, and search the game.Players for the users with plName.
4. We created a variable (money), to point to the players' money leaderstat. We took its current value and added five to it.

5. Then…wait…did we destroy the Part? Yup. No debounce here. The Part is going to be gone after we have touched it. (I'll explain in just a second.)
6. Last, we connected our Touched event to our function.

Now you can test this to see if it works by running the game and walking over the Part. It will work, and you will get five money. However, you will only get it one time.

So now what? Well, we aren't quite finished. Let's drag our MoneyGlob Part into the game.ServerStorage in the Explorer window. It will be safe there until we are ready to use it.

Now, inside the ServerScriptService in the Explorer window, create a new script and call it MoneyGlobDropper. This is going to be a script that will drop money globs, and set them as debris, so they will disappear after a set amount of time. Here's the code:

```
local moneyglob = game:GetService("ServerStorage")
.MoneyGlob
local Debris = game:GetService("Debris")

while(1) do
    wait()
    local newMoneyGlob = moneyglob:clone()
    local randX = math.random(-1000,1000)
    local randZ = math.random(-1000,1000)
    newMoneyGlob.Position = Vector3.new(randX,100,randZ)
    newMoneyGlob.Parent = workspace
    Debris:AddItem(newMoneyGlob,20)
end
```

You see we used some new ideas in this script. Like always, let's break it down line by line.

1. First we created a variable that points to our `Server-Storage` service, and gets our `.MoneyGlob` object. This will be the template for all the globs we make.
2. We then created a variable called `Debris` and got the Debris service to use for later. The debris service is great for cleaning up things like bullets that didn't hit a target, cars left behind on the street, exploded parts from a building, or anything else that would "junk up" the area after a while. You should add things like that to the Debris service and give them a TTL, or Time To Live.
3. Then in the main part of our script we created a **inf**. Loop. We added our **wait()** statement, and we should probably add a bit of a time delay, but for my example I didn't. Now with every iteration we create a new variable called `newMoneyGlob` by cloning our original `moneyglob` variable.
4. We created two variables called `randX` and `randZ`, and set their values by calling **math.random**. This will take in two variables: the lowest number and the highest number. In my case, -1000 and 1000. That's because we are going to set the position of our new MoneyGlob Part somewhere randomly in the world. We set the position by calling a **Vector3**.new and passing in our `randX` and `randZ` variables. I want the globs to look like they are falling from the sky, so the Y axis is set to 100.

5. Next we made sure we set the parent of our `newmoney` `glob` to Workspace so it will appear in the world.
6. Last, but far from least, we took our `newmoneyglob` and added it into the Debris service with a TTL of twenty seconds. If it's not picked up by then, it gets destroyed.

Now when we run our game, it gets much more interesting.

Roblox Corporation
WE CAN MOVE AROUND AND COLLECT GLOBS.

Now we can run around and collect all the globs we want! The script will continue to run, dropping more for us, and cleaning up the ones we don't take. You can use the money leaderstat to see if someone has enough money to purchase that sweet rocket launcher, or buy a new outfit, or maybe get a new axe. But here lies the next problem: What happens when the player leaves? Bye-bye, money. Bye-bye, new rocket launcher. To prevent tears and keep everyone happy, let's explore the DataStoreService.

THE DATASTORESERVICE

To start off, let me explain what the DataStoreService is. The DataStoreService saves information into a Roblox database on their servers. This data can be anything that we have previously discussed, from numbers to strings, objects, and even tables. We can use the DataStoreService to save a player's inventory, store, progress, or literally anything. A great example of this is how Lumber Tycoon 2 saves players' bases, money, and backpacks to a slot.

Here is an example of how the DataStoreService works, in the simplest way.

```
local DS = game:GetService("DataStoreService")
local Store = DS:GetDataStore("FirstStore")
local FirstKey = Store:GetAsync("FirstKey")

if FirstKey then
    print("Found: " .. FirstKey)
    print("Removing key so we can demo again.")
    Store:SetAsync("FirstKey", false)
else
    print("No key found. Making first key.")
    Store:SetAsync("FirstKey", "Heres the data")
end
```

Before I break it down, go ahead and run your game. The first time you run it, there are no "keys," which are individual player save files, so the system will generate one. The next time you run the game, it will find it and display it.

Please note, there is no actual way to delete data out of a DataStore, so what we have done is simply set the DataStore to **false** so when our code reads it, it will just return like if the key wasn't found in the first place. This is so we can test it again to be sure everything is correct. Okay, let's break the code down line by line.

```
local DS = game:GetService("DataStoreService")
```

Here, we created a variable called DS so we can reference the DataStoreService directly by just typing DS.

```
local Store = DS:GetDataStore("FirstStore")
```

In this line, we created a variable called Store to hold the a place for all the data in FirstStore. This could also be called Gold or XP. It's the table that holds all things related to that category. If we had named it Gold, it would hold everyone's gold.

```
local FirstKey = Store:GetAsync("FirstKey")
```

The variable "FirstKey" would be the scope or key of our data. It's the specific entry inside the DataStore we are looking for. Most of the time you will use something like "**player _ "** .. player.Id or something to that effect. This way you would get a unique key for every player to make an entry.

```
if FirstKey then
    print("Found: " .. FirstKey)
    print("Removing key so we can demo again.")
    Store:SetAsync("FirstKey", false)
```

Our first logical **if** says, "If our `FirstKey` variable has a value, then print out what that value is, and then set the value to **false**." The reason we are setting this value back to **false** is so we can test it more than once. To set a value that's in a DataStore we use `SetAsync`. It will take two arguments: the Key and the Value.

```
else
    print("No key found. Making first key.")
    Store:SetAsync("FirstKey", "Heres the data")
end
```

In the last portion of the code, if we did not find our `First-Key`, then we need to create the key with a value. Like I said before, this is the simplest way to explain how data is saved and retrieved.

COMPLEXED DATASTORESERVICE

In this section, I will be using an example that Roblox itself gives, because it is actually a cool and intelligent way to think about this technique. You can find the entire example at http://robloxdev.com/articles/Saving-Player-Data.

Before we get into the code, I will explain what the code is doing. In this example, we create a Module script. A Module script can be referenced by other scripts, which we can program functions to work with. (This keeps all the data consistent for any script that accesses the module.)

Inside the module, we create a table called Session. This table contains players' IDs and other information related to their save file. The module itself contains functions for manipulating the data, the autosave function, and the ability to load and save. Everything is wrapped up in a nice little bundle that you can use with other scripts.

Let's walk through the code, and I will explain each part and how it works. I will remove all of the comments to shorten this 100-line module. I highly encourage you to follow along by creating this script. Right-click on ServerScriptService in the Explorer window, and add a new Module script. Name the module PlayerStatManager. Here we go.

```
local PlayerStatManager = {}
local DataStoreService = game:GetService("DataStore
Service")
local playerData = DataStoreService:GetDataStore("Player
Data")
local AUTOSAVE_INTERVAL = 60
local DATASTORE_RETRIES = 3
local sessionData = {}
```

The first section of the script is comprised of all variables.

- PlayerStatManager is a reference to itself. This is what allows us to call functions and reference variables later from external programs. It is also the object we return at the end of this script.
- DataStoreService is our variable for holding the actual service.

- `playerData` is the variable that will hold our specific store of a player's file. Whenever we need to get or set data, we are going to use this variable.
- `AUTOSAVE_INTERVAL` is to be used when we run our autosave function. It will control how many seconds we will wait between saves before saving again.
- `DATASTORE_RETRIES` is used later in our autosave function. It will control how many times to retry a save if the save fails initially.

```
function PlayerStatManager:ChangeStat(player, statName,
changeValue)
    sessionData[player][statName] = sessionData[player]
    [statName] + changeValue
end
```

This function starts off with the name of our module (which was listed at the top of the script). When you create a Module script, and call it from another script, you assign it to a variable. For example, this one would be something like local `variable = require(game.ServerScriptService.PlayerStatManager)`. Then, whenever I would want to run the `ChangeStat` command, I would use the `variable:ChangeStat` and pass in the arguments of that specific player and the data attached to them. This would change the `sessionData` table value for that player in our Module script. (I hope I did not lose you there.) Basically, we are creating a function that we can call. Okay, deep breath. Let's continue.

```
local function dataStoreRetry(dataStoreFunction)
    local tries = 0
    local success = true
    local data = nil

    repeat
        tries = tries + 1
        success = pcall(function() data = dataStore
        Function() end)
        if not success then
            wait(1)
        end
    until tries == DATASTORE_RETRIES or success

    if not success then
        error("Could not access DataStore! Data might
        not save!")
    end
    return success, data
end
```

I promise it's not as confusing as it looks even though there are a lot of new concepts in this part. We will walk through it together.

- Just like our other functions, we start off by declaring the name of our function, dataStoreRetry. But then we pass in the argument dataStoreFunction. What exactly are we passing in? Well, we are going to pass in what the function does and not its name. This kind of function pass is an Anonymous Function.
- The next couple of lines are normal: Make variable tries, success, and data. Set the values.

- Now we have a Repeat Until loop. We have not discussed this. This function will loop the code until the condition is met at the end. It is guaranteed to run at least once, because it is not evaluated until the end of the loop. Don't get too caught up in the repeat. Treat it just like other loops we have discussed.

- During the loop, we increase our tries by one. We set our variable `success` to the result of `pcall`. A pcall is a Protected Call and will evaluate a function's results. If a function crashes, or errors out, the entire script usually stops. With a `pcall`, we can run that same function, then get the results and handle it ourselves without the script stopping. That's what is happening here. The argument that we passed into the entire function is a function itself. We evaluate that function inside the `pcall`, and `pcall` will return us two things. The first thing it returns is the result. Did the script run? `true` or `false`. The second thing that it passes back is a message string. If the call is good, we don't need to worry about the message, but if the call fails, then the message will tell us what happened. With our script, if it fails, the next part will wait for one second before trying again.

- At the end of the loop, whether we had a good call or a bad call after three tries, we send our results back to the developer. If there was an error, we use the error command to leave a big red message in the output window for the developer to see. We are passing back two variables, `success` and `data`. Don't let the label fool you, because `success` could equal `false`. The `dataStoreRetry` function is created before the other functions because it is used in the following functions. It should be easier from this point. I'll leave the comments in there just for labeling purposes.

```
-- Function to retrieve player's data from the
DataStore.
local function getPlayerData(player)
    return dataStoreRetry(function()
        return playerData:GetAsync(player.UserId)
    end)
end
```

This function will get the player data from the DataStore by calling the dataStoreRetry function and passing in an anonymous function. Okay, so the first thing to look at is the player argument of the function. We are passing in a player object, and using its UserId to call GetAsync. This is the main part of the function. (This isn't even the function we use to put the data into the session table. The getPlayerData is used in the setupPlayer Data function later.)

```
-- Function to save player's data to the DataStore.
local function savePlayerData(player)
    if sessionData[player] then
        return dataStoreRetry(function()
            return playerData:SetAsync(player.UserId,
            sessionData[player])
        end)
    end
end
```

The `savePlayerData` function is the same as the `getPlayerData` function with one change: Instead of `GetAsync`, we use `SetAsync`. With `SetAsync` we must pass in the value we want to save. In this case, it's the session entry for our player. So, in this case, we are not just saving a single key with a single value. We save a single key, the `player.UserId`, and a table of indexed data. It's a table within a table. The following illustration might clear things up a bit:

CodePrime8	Money	120
	Experience	32423
Another Player	Money	350
	Experience	12100
And Another Player	Money	10
	Experience	700

The values in the table are made up—this is just an example of a uniform table inside a table. No matter who we load the data for, we should have at least money and experience. That's what the `SetAsync` is doing. Just remember, we don't actually run `savePlayerData` directly. We will be doing it through other functions. Let's go through those.

```
local function setupPlayerData(player)
    local success, data = getPlayerData(player)
    if not success then
        -- Could not access DataStore, set session data
        for player to false.
        sessionData[player] = false
    else
        if not data then
            -- DataStores are working, but no data for
            this player
            sessionData[player] = {Money = 0, Experience
            = 0}
            savePlayerData(player)
        else
            -- DataStores are working and we got data for
            this player
            sessionData[player] = data
        end
    end
end
```

Here, we have the setupPlayerData function. It takes the argument of player, which is passed into our function from the PlayerAdded event that we will program later. In the first line, we see the first instance of our getPlayerData function that we created earlier.

Remember, the getPlayerData returns two things to us: A **true/false** to indicate if it ran correctly, and the information we requested. We store the returned information into two variables: success and data. We check to see if success was **true**. If it was not, we set our data to **false** to prevent it being used. If the `getPlayerData` worked we check to see if the data is good. If there is no data for the player, we create the `sessionData` entry with the player as the key, then set its value to a table of indexed values. This is the creation of the table within a table.

Now, because that's the first time that we have seen this player, we go ahead and immediately run the `savePlayerData` function to ensure that player's file will be in the DataStore next time the user joins. If the data was found, then we simply add it to our `sessionData` table.

THINK AHEAD

ONE PROBLEM WITH THIS METHOD OF SAVING DATA IS THAT IF YOU END UP ADDING ANYTHING MORE TO YOUR GAME, SAY ANOTHER LEVEL OR SAVEZONE, THEN IT WON'T BE THERE FOR ANYONE WHO ALREADY HAS A SAVE. IMAGINE THIS. YOUR GAME IS OUT FOR A WHILE, THEN LATER ON, YOU DECIDE TO ADD ANOTHER ASPECT TO YOUR PLAYER-DATA. WHEN SOMEONE WHO HAS ALREADY PLAYED THE GAME COMES IN, THE `else` FUNCTION HERE DOES NOT LOOK TO SEE IF THAT NEW VALUE THERE. I WOULD RECOMMEND SOME KIND OF CHECKING FOR YOUR DATA TO MAKE SURE THAT PLAYER'S FILE HAS THE SAME NUMBER OF KEYS AND VALUES THAT EVERYONE ELSE GETS WHEN THEY ARE FIRST STARTING.

Let's move to the autosave. WOOT WOOT!

```
-- Function to run in the background to periodically
save player's data.
local function autosave()
    while wait(AUTOSAVE_INTERVAL) do
        for player, data in pairs(sessionData) do
            savePlayerData(player)
        end
    end
end
```

The autosave function is pretty straightforward. We create a function that takes no arguments. We create a **while** loop that will perform a **wait** function for the time that we have given it. If your AUTOSAVE_INTERVAL at the top of your script is set to zero, then this function won't run and the game won't save automatically. The idea is to have this function running constantly and consistently while the game is running. To do this, we use a **for/in** loop with the sessionData (just like our apples and oranges example way back). This function will loop through the table and perform a savePlayerData function on each loop.

We are almost done! The last part is to connect everything up to its triggers, start the autosave, and return the module for use in the other scripts.

```
-- Bind setupPlayerData to PlayerAdded to call it when
player joins.
game.Players.PlayerAdded:connect(setupPlayerData)
```

We connect up our setupPlayerData to run when a player is added to the game. The Player variable is passed in from the .PlayerAdded function.

```
-- Call savePlayerData on PlayerRemoving to save
player data when they leave.
-- Also delete the player from the sessionData, as the
player isn't in-game anymore.
game.Players.PlayerRemoving:connect(function(player)
    savePlayerData(player)
    sessionData[player] = nil
end)
```

The player-removing bind is a little more complicated, but not much. Basically, when a player leaves for whatever reason, we want to make sure we save their data. Since the data is not bound to the player, and it resides in our `sessionData` table, we can save it at any time without the player being present or connected. Inside the connect, we create an anonymous function and pass in the player argument. We call the `savePlayerData` function, then we make that player's `sessionData` blank, or **nil**. This removes it from the sessionData.

```
-- Start running autosave function in the background.
spawn(autosave)
```

This is all of the code needed for autosave, we just need to make sure it runs. The **spawn** function will allow us to create a new Thread for the function to run on. We have not discussed threading, but think of it like this. We don't want our Module script or the script calling us to use up its resources on the **wait** function. And we certainly don't want to stop everything else that is going on in these scripts to wait for us to save. So we use **spawn**.

```
-- Return the PlayerStatManager table to external
scripts can access it.
return PlayerStatManager
```

The last thing to do is return the module to whoever called and requested it. You can run your game as is, but nothing is calling it at the moment, and nothing is changing its values. To do this, let's link up our leaderboard example with our PlayerStatManger module, then change the code for our globs to manipulate the players' data, not the board.

THE BIG PICTURE

I know this chapter is covering a lot, but it's really useful for taking your games to the next level. We now have a leaderboard, we have the ability to pick up some globs and make some money, and we have the ability to save our data so we can retrieve it once we leave. But it's all separate. Now we need to link it all up.

First, open up the PlayerStatManager module in the Explorer window. Add a new function at the very top before any other function and call it updateboard. It has to come first because it will be referenced on the ChangeStat function.

```
-- Function to Update the LeaderBoard
local function updateboard(player)
    for i,e in pairs(sessionData[player]) do
        player.leaderstats[i].Value = e
    end
end
```

Our new function will look at a player, then it will go through each value of that player's session data (Money, Experience) and set each leaderboard value to what it finds. Remember the apples and oranges? Same thing here—if there is a leaderboard stat name that does not correspond to our Session Data stat name, then this script will fail.

We will change the leaderboard in just a second. Right now, we need a couple of more changes to our module. Locate the `ChangeStat` function, and add `updateboard(player)`, just above the **end**. It should look like this:

```
function PlayerStatManager:ChangeStat(player, statName,
changeValue)
    sessionData[player][statName] = sessionData[player]
    [statName] + changeValue
    updateboard(player)
end
```

Now every time the `ChangeStat` function is called, it will automatically update the board. You must add the `updateboard` function in one more place. Locate the `setupPlayerData` function. At the end of this function between the last two **ends** add `updateboard(player)`. It will look like this:

```
    end
    updateboard(player)
end
```

Great! The module portion is done. Next up, we need to change the LeaderBoardScript. It should still be in your ServerScriptService in the Explorer window. Open it up. In here we used Gold and XP as our leaderboard names. We need to change these to Money and Experience. Keep in mind, you could change the module fields to match the leaderboard fields. Either way is fine; just make sure they match up. I should also note that if you have a status that will not be appearing on the leaderboard, and will still need to be changed/updated, you will have to change the `updateboard` function to skip it. Here is what my new Leader-BoardScript looks like:

```
local function AddBoard2Player(player)
    local board = Instance.new("Model",player)
    board.Name = "leaderstats"

    local money = Instance.new("IntValue",board)
    money.Name = "Money"
    money.Value = 0

    local xp = Instance.new("IntValue",board)
    xp.Name = "Experience"
    xp.Value = 0
end

game.Players.PlayerAdded:Connect(AddBoard2Player)
```

The only change on this is the names—everything else remains the same.

Time for the last part of the change. Open up the ServerStorage and look for the MoneyGlob. The MoneyGlob is currently changing the leaderboard stat and not the actual stat we are saving and working with. In fact, if you were to try and run it right now, you would get an error every time you tried to pick up a money glob. That's because the stat name has changed as well. Open the MoneyGiverScript inside the MoneyGlob and change it to the following:

```
local PlayerStatManager = require(game.ServerScript
Service.PlayerStatManager)
local me = script.Parent

local function GiveMoney(part)
    local hum = part.Parent:FindFirstChild("Humanoid")
    local plName = part.Parent.Name

    if hum then
        local player = game.Players:FindFirstChild(plName)
        PlayerStatManager:ChangeStat(player,"Money",5)
        me:Destroy()
    end
end

me.Touched:Connect(GiveMoney)
```

In our script we create a new variable PlayerStatManager that requires our module. This way, we can call our ChangeStat function from inside this script, and it will change the table of our module. Once you have this portion of the script complete, you should be able to run the game and start picking up money globs and getting money. If for some reason you are getting the error "attempt to index field '?' (a nil value)" then go to file and publish your game on Roblox. You can test it from the Roblox website instead.

Roblox Corporation
THE LEADERBOARD IS IN THE UPPER RIGHT-HAND CORNER.

FINISHING UP

I know this was a lot to digest, but it's worth the effort. Most games you create will need to have some form of saving. You have other options with the DataStoreService too:

- The ability to pull up a DataStore in an ordered list, so you can go over each record one by one and page through the entire store.
- The ability to pull up a single DataStore for multiple places in one Roblox game.

The other reason for this chapter is to walk you through an example of how each script will start to build on itself. You might write a script, just to have to go back some time later and change the way the script worked. In my own opinion, a script is never truly finished. I view it more as a living document that changes over time to fill the needs of the game.

PART 3

EXPERT MODE

CHAPTER 8

GAME ON

Before you start building, scripting, or making any part to a game, you need to plan it. There have been many times games have been published on Roblox with no idea about what the player is supposed to do. There's no consistent theme or overall feel for the game. These are bad games. They do not keep the user entertained or engaged, and will not be popular. I myself am guilty of this, so I can tell you how to avoid those mistakes. This chapter is completely dedicated to giving you the tools you need to decide what kind of game you want to make, write out your game into a storyboard, or work flow, and identify what components you are going to need to turn your game into a reality. We won't have much scripting for this chapter. The building and scripting will come after.

CHOOSING WHAT TYPE OF GAME TO MAKE

If you already have an idea for a game, get yourself a notebook and write it down. Keeping a running list of ideas will help make sure you don't forget any and will help you work out the details.

Here are some examples of the types of games we find on Roblox:

- **Obby:** One of the most commonly found type of game is an obby. "Escape the _____" tends to be very popular. This type of games is usually quick to make but does not have much replay factor. It can be fun but can get redundant quickly. So, unless you are going big like the Mega Fun Obby with more than 1,000 levels, keep these to a minimum.

- **Tycoons:** The next most common game that we see inside Roblox are Tycoons. The idea is you start with a piece of land, purchase some sort of dropper (a machine that drops building components), and make money over time to upgrade and buy more droppers. Some Tycoons do not fall into this style, but most have the same basic premise. Lumber Tycoon 2 and Theme Park Tycoon 2 have the same Make Money; Buy More concept, but do not involve template droppers. I find Tycoon games are more fun when they don't feel like dropper tycoons.

- **Simulators:** Simulator games commonly have you taking on the role of some type of job: a snow shoveler, treasure digger, or harvester. You go out and collect items with a limited availability, then sell them for money to purchase better equipment to go out and collect more items, faster. Although it doesn't look like it, Bird Simulator is the same concept.

- **PvP:** Player vs Player games can be seen in every shape and size. In my opinion, the ultimate PvP is Phantom Forces. In a PvP game, players can either be placed on teams or fend for themselves against everyone with the goal of defeating the other team or players. Rewards are based on eliminations, and are used to upgrade to better gear.

- **Role-Play:** In role-play games, the rules are a lot less defined by the game, and more make believe on the part of the player. Games like Adopt Me!, MeepCity, and Royale High fall into these categories. You still have tasks that will help you better your gear and homes, but the point is to role-play, and pretend with each other.

- **RPG**: RPG stands for role-playing game, but is much different from role-play games. In an RPG, you are usually fighting enemies that are other real people or computer-generated or non-playable characters known as NPCs. An RPG can be fantasy with dragons, futuristic with blasters, or somewhere between with modern-day items. What mostly defines these types of games is gaining experience points to level-up your character and complete a quest or task.

Not all games fall into these categories, but I wanted to point out some of the more common ones. There is no type of game that is better than any other type of game. It is all personal opinion. Does your game fall into one of these categories?

GAME THEMES

Does your game have an overarching theme? Make sure you define what that theme is, and have it set throughout the entirety of the game. For example, if you have a wizards-and-warriors type game style, don't go putting skateboards and laser pistols in the game. If it's a Western theme, don't put wands and flying broomsticks in the game. Keeping your game consistent will help the players engage and feel like they're really in your world. This is called immersion, and the better the immersion experience, the more likely a user will come back to play.

WHAT'S YOUR STORYLINE?

Grab your notebook again and write down how your world came to be. How did the player get to be...the player? Are they the hero of the story? Are they a member of an elite team? Are they a clone? Be sure to write down what the player's role is, who they are playing, and what challenges they must face. Different style games means different types of storylines. Some may not even have conflict. If that's the case, write that down. You need to have a clear understanding of what it is your players are going to be doing. The same process that you would use to write a book can be used to write a game story.

CHARACTER DEVELOPMENT

The next thing you need to do is write down what the characters of your game are. If you have NPCs, write them down. What are their names, what do they do (occupation), what is their back story, and what is their demeanor? Basically, you are carving out and shaping who the players and NPCs are, and how they act. You don't need a full lineage of their background or a complete life story, but you need enough information to help define what this character might do in a given situation.

Just like with the storyline, your game might not need character development. If you are making a game of 2D Tic-Tac-Toe, then I doubt you need to do any character development.

STORYBOARDING

Once you have your characters, theme, and storyline all planned out, you can create a storyboard. A storyboard is a step-by-step diagram or chart that shows where the players start, then takes them through each scene. If there is an ending to the game, then all scenes should eventually lead to the ending. You can think of a storyboard like a flowchart. I'll give one small example of what a General Store scene would look like drawn out in a rough storyboard/flowchart form.

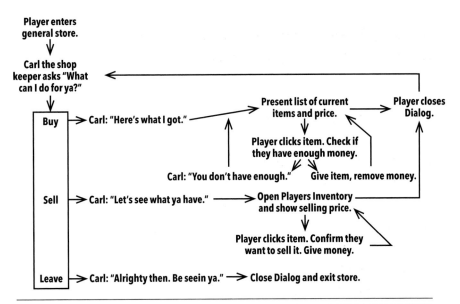

IN THIS SIMPLE EXAMPLE, WE CAN TRACE THE PATH OF WHAT THE CHARACTER IS DOING, HOW THE NPC IS RESPONDING, AND COVER ALL THE SITUATIONS THAT WE WILL HAVE TO PROGRAM LATER ON.

If it seems like your board/chart is getting too big, you might be putting too much information in it. Try to make the items part of the big picture rather than including every single detail.

MAKING IT REAL

At this point, you should have all the concepts of your game hashed out. You know what you are going to be making and what everything should look like. So to start, you should design the level. This could be an open area, a dungeon, or a flat playing board—whatever medium the players will be interacting with should be in place first.

CHECK OUT BLENDER 3D

I ENCOURAGE YOU TO DOWNLOAD BLENDER 3D FROM WWW.BLENDER .ORG. BLENDER 3D IS AN OPEN-SOURCE 3D CREATION STUDIO. IT IS FREE TO USE. I USE BLENDER TO CREATE CUSTOM MESH PARTS IN ROBLOX. IT IS FREE. WHEN I EDIT MY VIDEOS FOR YOUTUBE, I USE BLENDER. ONE HUNDRED PERCENT FREE. IT CAN BE USED TO MAKE REALISTIC IMAGES. COMPLETELY FREE. THERE HAVE BEEN ENTIRE MOVIES CREATED WITH JUST BLENDER. DID I MENTION IT WAS FREE? BLENDER IS AN EXTREMELY POWERFUL TOOL, BUT THERE IS A BIG TRADEOFF. IT IS COMPLICATED. I HAVE BEEN USING IT SINCE I FIRST DISCOVERED IT BACK IN 2000. SINCE THIS BOOK IS ABOUT ROBLOX AND NOT BLENDER, I WILL HOP OFF THE SUBJECT, BUT I HIGHLY ENCOURAGE YOU TO LOOK AROUND BLENDER'S WEBSITE AND RUN THROUGH SOME OF THEIR TUTORIALS.

TIPS FOR USING STUDIO

You will be building and creating things inside Studio. Here are some ideas to keep in mind as you work.

Save Often

Remember to save your work often. As you are building more and more onto your game, Roblox will autosave. Studio has been known to crash every once in a while, though, so keep saving manually too. There is nothing more frustrating than creating an awesome model of something, then having it entirely wiped because Studio crashed.

Use Folders

I cannot stress this enough. When you are building and creating, you will start to accumulate things. If you do not manage them early on, you have a difficult time keeping track of everything later. Here is what my sitting room game looks like.

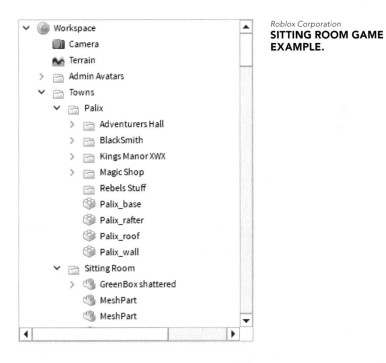

Roblox Corporation
SITTING ROOM GAME EXAMPLE.

You can see that each one of my buildings, as well as the items inside that building, are in their own folder. All the buildings in a town are in a Town folder, and so forth. Keep your main Workspace clear of any free objects. When you expand your Workspace, you should have a series of folders, not objects.

Use Union

When building, union things that go together as one object. For example, a chair will have four legs, one seat, two back posts, and three cross posts. You should union these into one object and call it Chair.

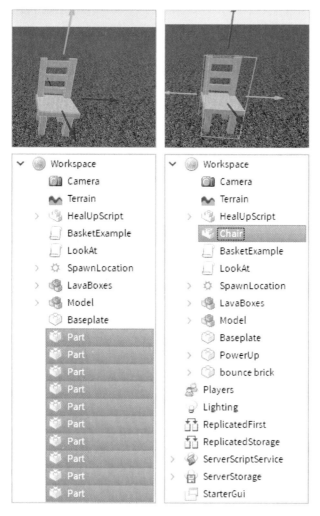

Roblox Corporation
USE UNION TO JOIN THESE PARTS.

Make Models

Make models out of unions. For example, if you have four chairs, a table, and a center piece, you should group these into one model and call it Dining Set. By creating models, you can start to manage areas without a bunch of copying and pasting. Also, if you build a single model that you are going to be using over and over, then you should export it as a model into your Models area.

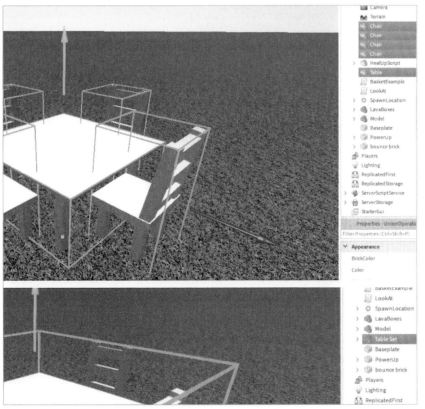

Roblox Corporation

EXPORTING A MODEL INTO THE MODELS AREA.

STARTING THE CODE

Whew! There were lots of things to do before even getting to code, right? Now that you have an idea of what is going to happen, how it looks, and a world to play in, it's time to get scripting. There are a few different ideas behind the scripting in games:

1. The first is a Game Controller script. This is a main script that runs on the server. It will control different aspects like rounds, manage players, select teams, and so forth. This script is the one that will be doing the majority of the work load. An example of this is Phantom Forces. The Game Controller watches for when players join, adds them to a team, controls the map selection keeps track of the time in game, and so on. Now Game Controller is not the only script by any means. The game itself has scripts inside the guns, on the menu items, in the player. The idea here is that one overall script is controlling the flow of the game while the other scripts are controlling different parts of the game.

2. Some types of games do not have or need a main script. MeepCity will be my example for this. The main game is an open world style game. Now there are mini games like Star Ball, and Kart Racing inside the game, but you should note that when you enter these areas, you are no longer in the main MeepCity game. You are transported into a different place. Another example of this is Jail-Break. There are different controller scripts for the Bank

Heist, Diamond Store, and Museum, but not an overall main controller script. You should be able to tell the difference between what a main script is handling and what a Player Manager script is handling. Like in our example of DataStorage, stats are handled by a different script, not the main controller script. So if your game uses rounds, a lobby, team selections or something along those lines, then start with the controller script.

MUSIC AND FOLEY

Background music is one of the most important aspects of a game. You can change the entire feel of a scene or game just by music. Roblox recently added a bunch of music from APM and has provided it for us developers to use. Be sure you use those options because of copyright laws. I won't go into the details, but basically you can't take a song that you hear on the radio and really like, then upload it to Roblox. It's illegal.

Choosing or making the right music for the right scene can transport the player from just playing a game to becoming immersed into their character. This is what you want.

Sometimes, actual music is not needed for a particular part or scene but other sounds could complement it. I'm talking about sounds like gentle rain falling, birds chirping, or the crackling of a campfire. These are all called Foley, or more commonly Sound Effects (SFX). Roblox provides some sound effects that are stored inside the player object themselves. You can view these by playing the game, then looking inside the player object. They are stored in the Head object.

Roblox Corporation
FINDING THE SPOT TO ADD SOUND IN THE HEAD OBJECT.

If you are going to create your own Foley sounds, I highly recommend getting a very nice directional condenser microphone. You should also create them in a sound-free or soundproof area. A program that you can use to create these masterpieces is Audacity. It is free to download and use. I love free stuff, don't you?

Walk through your game and take note of things that should have sound: opening doors, walking on metal, hitting a tree, swinging an axe. Also consider spaces...a chattering room of coffee drinkers in a coffee shop would have other sounds, like clinking of glasses, register ka-chings, and other environmental influences.

TESTING YOUR GAME

As you program each script, make sure you test it. Not just in Studio, but upload it, and see if it works the same way online. I have found many times that a script will work one way inside Studio, then completely different once I upload it. That's because the two environments are not the same, and the only true test is once it is up and running. For this reason, you will see a lot of bigger games that will have a main game that everyone is playing, and the developer will have a separate game that is used for testing and developing.

Do not publish untested scripts, especially if your game gets popular. This is also known as Testing in Production, or Deving in Production, and it's a huge no-no. So don't.

ASK A FRIEND TO HELP

A quick note about testing the game you make: You might not notice some kinks like another person would. So have someone else run through and test. Have them tell you want they would like to see, what happened when they did things, and if the scripts worked correctly. Let me tell you, I create applications, webpages, user interfaces, and server backends all day long. I will think a program is good, then all of a sudden someone puts in the word *zero* for an amount, and my entire program comes to a halt because it was looking for a number, not a word. That's why you should let someone else test.

PUBLISH

Once everything is done and working, it's time to put your game out there for the world to see. Advertising is a good way to send out the message that your game is available, but that takes some Robux cash money. You might not have it, so the best thing to do is to have your friends start playing it. Invite some people to come and play with you. They will invite their friends, and so forth. If you happen to know a YouTuber *cough* *cough*, you could always ask them to play the game. Huge disclaimer here: If a well-known YouTuber or streamer plays your game and you have not tested it and worked out the bugs, bad publicity could be devastating to how well your game will go over with the public.

UPDATES AND FIXES

Oh, you thought publishing was the end? Sorry, but you will need to keep up with the players. If you find people are gaining levels too quickly (or too slowly), you will need to adjust your code so players don't get bored.

At the same time, try not to release too many updates to your game either. If you are sending out a new update every day, the players are not going to be able to keep up. A nice rate to keep things interesting is one update about every two weeks. This keeps the interest, and has a lasting effect. What can you update? Maybe add a new item or a new event. If your game is in the alpha stage, pass out an alpha item that can be obtained only during the alpha stage of the game.

Finally, read and listen to your comments section. If you see a trend start happening, like "saves won't load" or "I lost all my inventory when X happened," then try to respond to them as quickly as possible and fix the mistake(s).

FINISHING UP

In this chapter, we have gone over the concepts of creating a game. I hear players asking all the time, "Can you help me make a game?" and I know that they don't understand the process that goes into making it. The programming behind a game is only a small portion of the game as a whole. Simply being a great programmer will not win you the next RDC challenge, or a Bloxy Award. Being creative and innovative and thinking through your game from beginning to end before you script will be the key to your game's success.

CHAPTER

9

LET'S MAKE A GAME

n this chapter, we are going to make a game, from start to finish, using the methods we just discussed. That's right. Now, because of restrictions in the book, it's not going to be a super elaborate game. We are going for the easiest and simplest game: an obby. BUT because I am me, and I like to hide things, our obby is going to have some MAJOR twists in it. My obby should already be out and playable by the time this book is published. Let's get started by planning everything out. This is going to be fun.

THE PLAN

This obby is going to be a dungeon-style theme. Players will have to run down long corridors, avoid traps, make death-defying leaps, and run along cobblestone mazes. What can I say? I grew up playing Dungeons and Dragons. Running the long mazes and gauntlets were my favorite parts, besides the village area where you got to hang out and visit the local shops. Hmm. That sounds pretty cool too. Let's add a local village at the beginning of our obby, before you go running down into the maze.

I also want this obby to have some very special properties:

1. Any user who joins will only have one chance every twenty-four hours to try to beat the obby. If the timer runs out or if they die, they are kicked out. When they try to log back in, it will inform them of how long they have to wait until they can get back in. This should prevent them from attempting the maze multiple times in a row and presents a very interesting twist to how a game can be played.

2. We give the user only five minutes to complete the obby. Finishing the obby normally will grant you a badge, but not *the badge*. The hidden, super-secret squirrel badge will have to be activated by performing various tasks throughout the obby.

CHARACTER DEVELOPMENT

The players are themselves. They have come to my world to look for the egg that I have hidden. We are not going to allow any outside items into the game, so we will need to restrict that. Also, because of the nature of the game, we are going to have to check for any users who are under a week old. Young users could mean some players have created new characters so they can cheat and try more than once a day.

One other main character is going to be my avatar. When the player first gets into the world, my avatar will give a monologue to the player that welcomes them to the game and gives them details of how they are supposed to play. This speech has two goals:

1. The main purpose is to instruct the player on the game details and rules.
2. The second purpose is sneakier: to waste their time. The more time we can get the player to stay put, the less time they will have to complete the obby. The last part of my dialog will be informing them that the timer already started.

We can add a few other NPCs that will talk in the main area just before you start, but they won't have any kind of main role. They are there to distract the player.

STORYLINE/STORYBOARD

Let's go through our process of what is happening and how the player will play the game. I love storyboarding. There isn't really a storyline, because it's an obby, but I will make one up.

The village is a small settlement I came across on my travels. While the village itself is quite small, it did have a large secret. Underneath the village were tunnels built by dwarves long ago. Most of the tunnels have fallen into disarray, and are now just crumbling piles of stone and earth. Any treasures the dwarves may have hidden in the chambers have long been stolen or buried. Except one: a cursed item. An evil item. The hidden thing was placed in the dwarves' tunnels by one of their own.

This dwarf had sought the help of a wizard to help him take over as the dwarves' leader. He didn't want to hurt anyone, just move them out of the way so he could take over. The wizard granted the little dwarf his wish, and gave him a glowing orb he called The Orb of Praventionis (prevention). The dwarf took the orb to the center of the tunnels and activated it. He did not expect what happened next. Everyone in the tunnel was expelled and pushed out. When they tried to return, they could not enter. The orb's power extended beyond the reach of just the tunnels. It affected the village and the area around it as well. Any new travelers who came to the village would be able to stay only for a short period of time before they, too, were sent back to where they began their travel to the village. This includes you, traveler. You have but a moment to find and retrieve the orb. I expect your time began to count down the moment you arrived. Seek the orb and stop it, so that the villagers can return to their tunnels and newcomers can travel here to recreate their wonders.

Wow, okay, that came out a lot cooler than I thought it would. I just started writing and boom. Storyline. Thank you, ADHD, once again, for having my back on this one. Let's get to building our obby.

CREATING THE WORLD

To start, I will head out to Roblox, and go to my Create tab, and click on Create New Game.

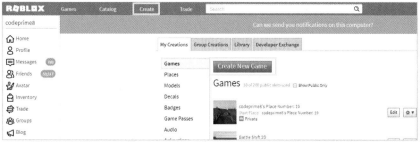

Roblox Corporation
CREATING A NEW GAME.

Roblox has a lot of templates that we can choose from to help us get started. Because my game starts in a village, I'm going to use the Village template.

Roblox Corporation
LET'S SELECT THE VILLAGE TEMPLATE.

As for the rest of the tabs, I'll change the name of the Basic Settings tab to The Orb of Praventionis. In Description, I will type in my storyline. I will also change the Genre to Adventure. Moving along to the Access tab, I'm going to:

- Make the game available to all devices.
- Set the Maximum Player count to 1. We want only one player at a time in the game.
- Uncheck the VIP servers, as there is only room for one player at a time. Because this is a one-player game, I won't need to set any of the Advanced Settings and will leave them as default. Hit Create Game.

CHECK OUT THE SCENERY

Once the game shows up in your Games list, click on Edit to open Studio. When Studio opens, the first thing I usually do is look at the Workspace. I expand it out and look at the folders. Then I click on the main window and fly around the world using W, S, A, D for movements; E and Q for up and down; and the right mouse button for turning the camera.

Roblox Corporation
CHECKING OUT OUR VILLAGE.

PLACING AN AVATAR

My avatar is going to be the one to greet the player. To get our avatar into the game, press Play in Studio. Then once the game is running, look in the Workspace for our avatar model. It will be the same name as your avatar. Select the model in the Explorer window, then right-click Copy. Now stop the game by hitting the red Stop button at the top of the screen. After the game stops, right-click on Workspace, and select Paste Into. Your model will now appear in the world. Be sure to drag the avatar from where it is in the Explorer window into the Info NPCs folder.

Next we need a starting spot for our player. Under the Model tab, click on Spawn. I'm going to move the spawn pad and my avatar to the road just in front of the Sign Post.

Roblox Corporation
LET'S SPAWN RIGHT NEAR THE SIGN POST.

Change the properties of the pad by clicking on it, which will bring up the Properties window. In that window, set Transparency equal to 1.0, and CanCollide to False by unchecking the box next to it. You can also change the property of the Decal inside the spawn pad. Do this by expanding the Spawn Location menu option in the Explorer window and clicking Decal.

Next, remove all of the Info Bubbles located inside the Info NPC's folder. We won't be using them. In the main window there is a Some Place label on the sign post. Hold down the ALT key on your keyboard and click on the Some Place label. You can now change it from the Explorer window. Expand the Sign Post object. Then expand the Direction object and the SurfaceGui object. From there, click on the TextLabel option and change the text in the Properties window to The Tunnels.

Roblox Corporation

HERE'S WHERE YOU CAN CHANGE THE TEXT ON THE SIGN POST.

BUILDING THE TERRAIN

Since our game is an obby first, let's get to building it. The sign is pointing to a nice little rocky area. I'm going to switch to the Terrain Editor, and start digging a tunnel down into the earth.

Roblox Corporation
OUR PLAN FOR THE TUNNEL LOCATION.

Using the Subtract tool and selecting the block shape, I dig an angled tunnel into the rocks just behind the first rocks seen. Once I have a little bit of a tunnel, I use the Regions tool to select a rectangular area, and delete it from the ground below.

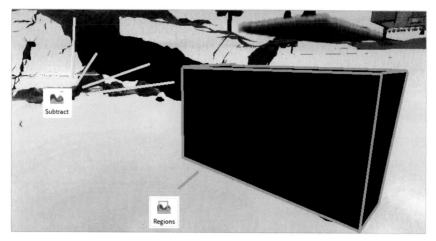

Roblox Corporation
THIS IS A FASTER WAY TO BUILD THE TUNNEL.

This is our first chamber. To keep our Workspace clean, create a new folder inside Workspace called Tunnels. We are going to place things into different folders so we can keep everything nice and tidy.

Did you notice that it is pitch-black down there? While we are building, select Lighting, from the Explorer window and change Ambient to 255,255,255. This will light it up so we can see. Whew! Let's build some walls around the first chamber and make them look like the walls of a castle:

- Click on the Part button at the top of the screen to add a new brick. Before you do anything else, go to Properties and check the box next to Anchored. Using the Move tool, position it next to one of the chamber walls so that it's just barely touching the wall itself.

- Now use the Scale tool, and drag the edges to the width and height of the chamber.
- In the Properties window, change the Material to Brick. What I like to do at this point is use CTRL + D to duplicate that wall. This way all I have to do is use the Move tool, and put it on the opposite side.
- Duplicate the wall a third time and use the Scale tool to make a roof and a floor. Now we have something like this:

Roblox Corporation
CURRENT STATE OF OUR CHAMBER.

Next, let's add a lava floor.

- Make a new Part and move it to the bottom of the chamber.
- Check the box next to Anchored in the Properties window. Use the Scale tool to fill up the bottom of the chamber.
- For my floor, I change the Material to Corroded Metal. I also select the brightest red from the color wheel.
- Now here's something cool. I click on the lava floor Part in the Explorer window, and add a Surface Light from

the drop-down menu. In the Surface Light Properties, I change the color from white to red, and set the Face to Top. Face is which side of the part you want the light to come out. I turned off the Ambient Light option from the Lighting menu in the Explorer window so I could take a picture of what it looks like.

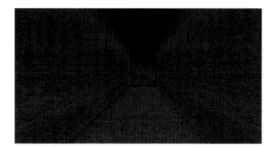

OUR COOL-LOOKING LAVA FLOOR.

I also added a script to the floor, and dropped it in. You can too, if you like. I named it LavaFloor.

```
function kill_player(part)
    local hum = part.Parent:FindFirstChild("Humanoid")

    if hum then
        hum.Health = 0
    end
end


script.Parent.Touched:Connect(kill_player)
```

Creating Chamber 1

We need to build some platforms for our players to jump across, but I don't want them to look like they are just floating in the air. I want it to look like an old bridge that has crumbled away. To do this, I'll make a small staircase at the front by creating new Parts, then use some negative Parts to combine with them. All the Parts are going to be concrete and gray. I use the Scale tool to manipulate the size of the Part. When it's the length and size that I like, I press CTRL + D to duplicate it, and make the next. Scaling and moving, I finally end up with six blocks, like this.

Roblox Corporation
BRIDGE STAIRS AFTER WE CHANGE THE DIMENSIONS AND SCALE.

I don't want my stairs to look clean-cut like this, so I create some smaller Parts that we are going to use to "cut" the stairs. I place them along the edge and make sure they look good. Once they are in place, I press the Negate button under the Model tab at the top of the screen. This will turn the Parts red. Keep in mind that once a Part is negative you cannot scale it the same way as before.

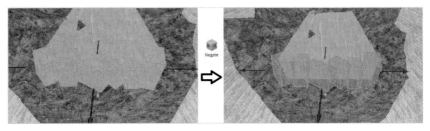

Roblox Corporation
USING THE NEGATE BUTTON TO TAKE CHUNKS OUT OF THE STAIRS.

Now I select all of the negative Parts and the stairs. By pressing the Union button at the top of the screen (or pressing CTRL + SHIFT + G) all of the negative Parts will cut out portions of the positive bricks. You can use negatives to carve out very cool designs and patterns.

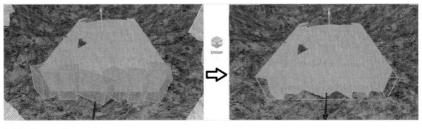

Roblox Corporation
THE END RESULT.

Next up, let's make some pillars for the platforms. Using the same technique, I'm going to use two Parts, one bigger than the other, and a cylinder. Turn the cylinder on its side, and make it the same width as the smaller Part. Move the cylinder through the first Part, make it negative and union all three Parts together to complete the pillar.

Roblox Corporation
**MAKING A PILLAR
IN THREE STEPS.**

We will duplicate these pillars a couple times through our chamber, and place them evenly throughout (except for the last one, which will be closer to the wall). I also want to turn one of them so it looks like it has fallen. I will also place some platform tops on the first three. Plus, I'll make the last one look tilted, as though it has fallen as well.

Roblox Corporation
**THE ROW OF
PILLARS.**

Now for the sneaky part. This run, as a normal obby, would be fast, but here's the problem. The player is going to have one chance a day to navigate this course in five minutes. It's not going to be fun just blasting through it and completing it the first day. So, I am going to make it more interesting. I am going to place some traps on Pillars 2 and 5. The top platform on Pillar 2 we are going to make slide and fall as soon as the player jumps on it. To do this, I make a second platform top, rotate it forward by 15 degrees, and make it negative. Selecting the pillar and the negative Part, I union them together. Make sure you do not union the first platform block.

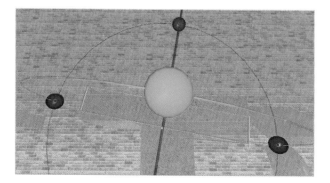

Roblox Corporation
ROTATING THE PILLAR.

The pillar should now have a slight slant to allow the platform to "fall" forward. Now for my favorite part: script it! Add a new script to the gray platform. Here is the code to make it fall when a player jumps on it. I named the script Platform_crack.

```
local canfall = true
this = script.Parent
BrickSound = Instance.new("Sound",script.Parent)
BrickSound.SoundId = "rbxassetid://1679240122"
```

```
this.Touched:Connect(function(part)
    if part.Parent:FindFirstChild("Humanoid") and
    canplay then
        canfall = false
        BrickSound:Play()
        this.Anchored = false
        wait(5)
        this.Anchored = true
        script:Destroy()
    end
end)
```

The variable `canfall` is our debounce. This is a way I refer to the part the script is in. BrickSound is a new instance of a sound that we place into the Part. I found a "Brick Breaking" sound made by Roblox in the Roblox library.

Roblox Corporation

HERE'S HOW TO GRAB THE BRICK-BREAKING SOUND AVAILABLE FOR US IN THE ROBLOX LIBRARY.

You could use the Get button to pull the sound into your inventory, so you can insert it. However, what I like to do is create a new Sound from the Workplace menu in the Explorer window, and set the SoundID to the number found in the URL. This one is 1843359148. To use it we set SoundID to "`rbxassetid://1679240122`". This tells Roblox where to get the sound. Last, I created an anonymous check for the sound. We are doing the same touch check that we have performed before. If it's a player, play the sound, unanchor the part.

It's here I do something different. That script is done, so I don't want to keep it around anymore. Anchor the part wherever it lands after five seconds, then destroy the script using the `:destroy()` function.

I tested this a few times, and it works quite well. Now, I need to make sure that the user can actually get to the next pillar. By default, I'm saying that players can walk up anything on a slope of 85 degrees or less. (That's steep, but works for this game.) For the next pillar, I leave everything anchored down, and just rotate the pillar and the platform. I make sure the angle is steep enough to walk up. So, the player will fall, but can land on the side of the pillar, then walk up to the slanted platform, and on to the next jump.

Roblox Corporation
THE PATH THE PLAYER CAN TAKE.

Pillar 5 we are going to have "fall" forward. If the player attempts the last jump without allowing the pillar to fall, they won't make it. To do this we move to the bottom of Pillar 5. Make a negative Part the same as before, and union it at 15 degrees on the bottom. The upward slant should be facing the back of the chamber.

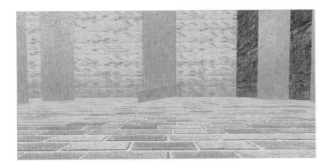

MOVING THE BOTTOM OF PILLAR 5.

To save time, copy the Platform_crack script. Then right-click on the falling pillar from the Explorer window, and use Paste Into. It should work the exact same way as the platform from the first one. Great! I think our first chamber is all done!

Creating Chamber 2

I pull out my Terrain editor once more and use the Regions tool to cut out a hallway. I want to make sure it's smaller so it will look like a passage.

The second chamber is going to be a gas-filled room that will start to do damage to the player over time while they are running through it. Using the Paint tool in the Terrain Editor, I select Pavement in the Material menu and go around the room to make it look like it's been built instead of a natural cut in the ground.

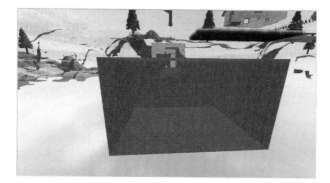

This gives the room a nice feel. Select the first part of the bridge from Chamber 1 and copy it. Drag it over to the exit of Chamber 1 and rotate it (turn it around) on the Y-axis by 180 degrees.

I created a new folder in the Workspace, and called it Chamber 2. Then I create a single Part that I will use for the template in this room. In the Properties window, I use Medium Stone Grey as the color, and Concrete for the texture. Be sure to anchor the Part. I also make sure my Rotate and Move are set to 15 degrees and one stud in the Model tab at the top of the screen. This way, every new Part I create and move around is on the same unit scale as the last one.

I don't want the player to be able to just jump or fall down the stairs. To prevent them from doing this, I create another Part, and select Transparent from the Properties window so that the player can't see it. You can see them selected in the image, but not when the game is running.

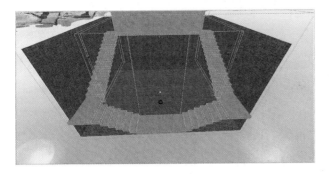

Roblox Corporation
THE LOCATION OF OUR STAIRCASES.

Later, I will add a sound and a box to this room that covers the whole area. We are going to program this box to be the poisonous gas.

This room is also going to have a door, but that door can be opened only by pulling a lever at the back of the chamber. This door will lead to Chamber 3, where our orb will be waiting.

I will go ahead and create the lever first. I am going to use four Parts for the lever. The first is going to be square. The second, third, and fourth will be cylinders. Scaling, rotating, and moving the pieces into place, this is what I finally came up with. Make sure the down lever is transparent. The names are LeverBase, LeverGear, LeverHandleUp, and LeverHandleDown. This will be important later, so make sure you name them now. Once you are done, press CTRL + G to union them. Name the union Lever in the Workplace.

Roblox Corporation
OUR LEVEL UNION.

Using the Negate technique from earlier, I create a gate that will function with the lever. I create the arch for the door first by using one of the stairs as my base. Once I have it to the correct size, I make two additional Parts, change one to a cylinder, and make them both negative. These will be the arch and passage part of our gate.

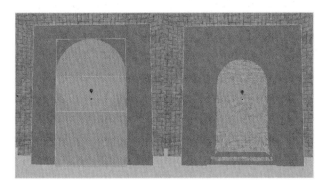

Roblox Corporation
**THE GATE,
BEFORE AND
AFTER USING
THE NEGATE
TECHNIQUE.**

Nice. Now I will take a cylinder, and make some large bars with square crossbars. The fastest way to do this is to create one of each Part, then duplicate and move. I used granite for the material, and a bright green for the color for each Part. Once I have them all where I like them, I press CTRL + G and union them up into a model that I will call Jade Gate.

Roblox Corporation
**THE FINAL JADE
GATE.**

The last thing I will need for this room is the gas itself. There is no modeling for it, as the player will not see it. This is just an indicator of where the gas will be. Make a new Part. Name it Gas and scale it so it covers the entire room, and stops at the entrance and the gate. Nothing more to do, until we come back to program it. Make sure the Part is 0.5 transparent so you can still see the chamber inside. This will make it easier to move around and scale accordingly.

You may have noticed that I had already cut out the tunnel to Chamber 3. I used the Region tool again, and cut straight back behind the arch. Inside, I painted the walls with brick so they look different than the other two chambers. You could use whatever material you want, just make sure that it transitions nicely. In this chamber, we will place the orb.

YOUR OBBY SHOULD BE LONGER

IT MAY SEEM LIKE THIS IS A SHORT OBBY, AND YOU'RE RIGHT. TRUST ME, YOU SHOULD MAKE OBBYS MUCH LONGER THAN WHAT I HAVE DONE HERE. I AM MAKING MINE SHORTER BECAUSE IT HAS TO FIT IN THIS BOOK, AND BECAUSE OF THE TIME CONSTRAINTS WE'RE PLACING ON PLAYERS.

Creating Chamber 3

Make a new folder in the Workspace called Chamber 3. Add a new sphere Part into it. This is going to be the center of the orb. I am going to make it the color blue and the material neon.

Once I have it positioned it where I like it, I create a second sphere to go around the outside. This one is going to be made out of glass, and the color will be white. I am also setting the Transparency to 0.5 so we can see the blue orb inside it. Lastly, I add a Point Light inside the blue sphere by opening the Part drop-down menu in the within the Workspace. This is because it's going to be dark down here. I want the orb to be seen from the other side of the gate in Chamber 2. That's it!

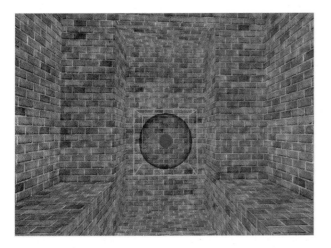

Roblox Corporation
HERE'S OUR ORB.

Whew! That was A LOT of building. Next up, we have to code everything and make it work. Let's do this.

PROGRAM THE WORLD

Let's piece together the code we need to get this game working.

INTRODUCING THE GAME TO PLAYERS

To start us off, I want my avatar to start speaking to the player as soon as they arrive. I am going to record my own dialog using a program called Audacity. Audacity is a free program for recording and mixing sounds. You can record and upload your own audio if you like. I will make a recording of the following for my dialog.

> Welcome, traveler, to the Village of Codin (pronounced Co-deen). This village has a great curse on it. Long ago, a dwarf by the name of Henlex activated a magical orb in the tunnels below us. The orb forces everyone out of the tunnels and the village, sending them back to where they traveled from. The orb will not let them return on the same day that they were forced out. This includes you, traveler. I need you to find the orb, and deactivate it. You will have only five minutes to get to the orb. By the way... that time started when you arrived. You will not be able to see in the tunnels, so I will cast a Light spell on you while you travel. Hurry!

Now to set up our code. Find your avatar in the Info NPCs folder. Click on the expand arrows, and find the part named Head. Add a script, and name it Opening Dialog. Here is the code.

```
local Dialog = Instance.new("Sound",script.Parent)
Dialog.SoundId = "rbxassetid://2358606830"
wait(5)
Dialog:Play()

while Dialog.Playing do
    wait()
end

for k,player in pairs(game.Players:GetChildren()) do
    local player _ head = player.Character.Head
    blah = Instance.new("PointLight",player _ head)
end
```

Here's what that code does:

- I created a variable called Dialog and set it to a new instance of a sound. The parent of that sound is the same parent as our script. I set the "SoundId" to rbxassetid://2358606830, which is the sound that I uploaded for this dialog.
- After a five-second wait, we call the :Play() function of the dialog so it starts to speak as soon as the world is loaded. The player should be able to hear the dialog start.
- Our next statement is a **while** loop. This will cause the script to wait until the dialog sound is finished playing to continue.
- In the last section of this code, I used a **for/in/do**, loop. This will go through all of the players and add a Point Light to their heads. That's because our tunnel is dark.

THE CONTROLLER SCRIPT

Next, we need to write the Controller script. This is the script that will be checking to see if the player had logged in before, how long ago it was, if they die, keep track of time, and play initial background music. Yeah—it's kind of an important script.

To start, I add a new script to the ServerScriptService and name it TheOrbsCurse. There's A LOT in this script. Because of that, I have added comments to help you recognize different parts and what they do. Deep breath.

```
--[[
This is the script that will look at the player's last
login
1) If the player has never logged in, or it's been more
than 24 hours, call SetAsync to store the current time
2) if the player has logged in before, see if it's
within the last 24 hours
3) if the player has logged in, and it's been less then
24 hours, kick.
4) if the player dies, or leaves while they are here,
kick
--]]

local DSS = game:GetService("DataStoreService")
local DS = DSS:GetDataStore("LastLogin")

local timeout = 86400 --86400 is default
local timetowin = 300 --300 is default

local OrbBadge = 2124427099
local FriendBadge = 2124427100
```

```lua
local CanTouchOrb = true

local BadgeService = game:GetService("BadgeService")

function checkLastLogin(player)
    --check to see if my egg is still hidden.
    local EggFound = DSS:GetDataStore("EggFound")
    local EggWinner = EggFound:GetAsync("Egg")

    if EggWinner then
        print(EggWinner, "has found the egg already.")
    else
        print("The egg is still hidden")
    end

    --add background music once the PlayerGui is there
    player:WaitForChild("PlayerGui")
    local music = Instance.new("Sound",player.PlayerGui)
    music.SoundId = "rbxassetid://1837720187"
    music:Play()
    music.Looped = true
    music.Name = "BackgroundMusic"

    --get the current time
    local currenttime = os.time()

    --pull the user's data for the last time they
    logged in
    local myLastLogin = DS:GetAsync(player.UserId)

    --If a time was found, let's check it.
    if myLastLogin then
```

```
    --Check to see if the last time they logged in
    was over 24 hours ago.
if (myLastLogin + timeout) > currenttime then

    --Time since last login is less than 24
    hours. Display a message and kick from game.
    print("Login found but it was less then 24
    hours.")
    msg = Instance.new("Message",workspace)
    msg.Text = "You still have " .. (myLastLogin
    + timeout) - currenttime .. " seconds before
    you can login again."
    player:Kick("You still have " .. (myLastLogin
    + timeout) - currenttime .. " seconds before
    you can login again.")
else
    --The user has been away longer than 24
    hours. Update their new time.
    print("Login found, and they have waited long
    enough.")
    DS:SetAsync(player.UserId, currenttime)
end
else --If the time wasn't found, create them a new
entry equal to current time.
    print("No login found. creating new.")
    myLastLogin = currenttime
    DS:SetAsync(player.UserId, currenttime)
end

--wait for Players avatar to appear in the world.
local char = workspace:WaitForChild(player.Name)
```

```lua
--Add a hook to the player. If they die, we kick
them from the game.
player.Character.Humanoid.Died:connect(function()
    print("You died")
    player:Kick("You have died. You must wait to
    return.")
end)

--Wait for the time to expire.
wait(timetowin)

--If it has been longer then the time we allow,
kick them from the game.
print("Took too long")
player:Kick("You have run out of time.")
end

--Function for when someone touched the orb at the end.
function OrbWin (part)

    --check for humanoid, and if we can touch the orb.
    if part.Parent:FindFirstChild("Humanoid") and
    CanTouchOrb then
        CanTouchOrb = false --Set the orb so it can't be
        touched again.

        --get the player, from the PlayerObject
        local player = game.Players:FindFirstChild(part
        .Parent.Name)
```

```lua
--Make a call to the badge service to see if
they have the orbbadge already.
local success, message = pcall(function()
    hasBadge = BadgeService:UserHasBadgeAsync
    (player.UserId, OrbBadge)
end)

--error checking.
if not success then
    warn("An error occurred while checking for
    badges: " .. tostring(message))
    return
end

--If the user does not have the OrbBadge, then
let's give it to them.
if hasBadge == false then

    print("Got the Orb badge")

    --check to see if the player has background
    music already.
    if player.PlayerGui:FindFirstChild
    ("BackgroundMusic") then
        player.PlayerGui.BackgroundMusic:Destroy()
    end

    --play some victory music. (happy song)
    Music = Instance.new("Sound", player.PlayerGui)
    Music.SoundId = "rbxassetid://1843404009"
    Music.Name = "BackgroundMusic"
    Music:Play()
```

```
--display message letting them know they won.
msg = Instance.new("Message",workspace)
msg.Text = "You saved the town, and got
the Orb."
BadgeService:AwardBadge(player.UserId,
OrbBadge)
else
    --If the user has already got the Orb Badge...

    --check to see if my egg is still hidden.
    local EggFound = DSS:GetDataStore("EggFound")
    local EggWinner = EggFound:GetAsync("Egg")

    --checks if the egg was already found, if so
    exit the function.
    if EggWinner then
        print("The egg has already been found")
        msg = Instance.new("Message", workspace)
        msg.Text = "Sorry, " .. EggWinner .. " has
        already found the egg."
        return
    end

    --See if the player is carrying an Apple in
    their backpack. (not in their hand)
    if player.Backpack:FindFirstChild("Apple") then

        --check to see if this player is already
        my friend.
        if player:IsFriendsWith(119529626) then
            print("Already friends with CodePrime8.")

            --play some goofy music.
```

```lua
if player.PlayerGui:FindFirstChild
("BackgroundMusic") then
    player.PlayerGui.BackgroundMusic:
    Destroy()
end

Music = Instance.new("Sound", player.
PlayerGui)
Music.SoundId = "rbxassetid://1839740301"
Music.Name = "BackgroundMusic"
Music:Play()

--Display the message letting them know
they are already my friend.
msg = Instance.new("Message", workspace)
msg.Text = ":D You are already my friend."
return
else
    --Egg available, not friend, has item.

    print("WinEvent Trigger")

    if player.PlayerGui:FindFirstChild
    ("BackgroundMusic") then
        player.PlayerGui.BackgroundMusic:
        Destroy()
    end

    --play some EPIC MUSIC!
    Music = Instance.new("Sound", player.
    PlayerGui)
    Music.SoundId = "rbxassetid://1847440957"
    Music.Name = "BackgroundMusic"
    Music:Play()
```

```
                    --Show the player they won!
                    msg = Instance.new("Message", workspace)
                    msg.Text = "YOU WON MY EGG!!!"

                    --Give out the badge
                    BadgeService:AwardBadge(player.UserId,
                    FriendBadge)

                    --Update the EggWinner so no one else
                    can get it.
                    EggFound:SetAsync("Egg", player.Name)

                end
            else
                --If the user did not have the item needed.
                print("Hmm.. missing something.")
                msg = Instance.new("Message", workspace)
                msg.Text = "Hmm. Seem to be missing
                something."
                wait(5)
                msg:Destroy()
            end
        end
    end
end

game.Players.PlayerAdded:Connect(checkLastLogin)
game.Workspace["Tunnels"]["Chamber 3"]["The Orb"]
["outerOrb"].Touched:Connect(OrbWin)
```

I know, right? Let's go through it.

At the top, I made a large comment about what I wanted the script to do. Next, I declared my DataStoreService and

`DataStore` variables to use. I set a `timeout` variable equal to the number of seconds in twenty-four hours (a full day). Then I set a `TimeToWin` equal to the number of seconds in five minutes.

Now, the `badge` numbers I got from the badges I uploaded for my game. If you would like to create a badge, go to the Create tab on Roblox.com. On the left side there is a Badges tab. Click on it. BEFORE YOU DO ANYTHING, make sure you select the correct game on the drop-down box. I have wasted Robux before because I had the wrong game selected. Next, choose a file to upload. Your image has to be 150x150 pixels. Look for the "Don't know how? Click here" link for a tutorial and a downloadable template so you can make your own. Once you have your picture selected, name your badge, give it a catchy description, then upload. When you click on your badge, the BadgeID will appear in the URL at the top.

Roblox Corporation
YOU CAN SEE INFORMATION ABOUT YOUR BADGE AND THE ID IS IN THE URL.

Next we define a debounce called `CanTouchOrb` and set it to **true**. A `BadgeService` variable will hold our BadgeService for later. The function `checkLastLogin` is vital. Read through the comments for this script to fully understand what each section is doing. Here's a general idea of what this section of the script does:

- It adds some music to the player's "music-player GUI" so they can hear it playing.

WHAT IS GUI?

GUI STANDS FOR GRAPHICAL USER INTERFACE. THE GUI IS A WAY TO COMMUNICATE INFORMATION TO THE PLAYER. MUSIC-PLAYERS ARE ONE TYPE OF GUI THAT ALLOWS PLAYERS TO LISTEN TO THEIR OWN MUSIC WHILE PLAYING GAMES. DEVELOPERS CAN ALSO SEND MUSIC FROM THEIR GAME TO THE PLAYER'S GUI SO THAT GAME-SPECIFIC MUSIC WILL BE HEARD AT THE APPROPRIATE TIME IN A GAME.

- It gets the current time. The function `os.time()` returns how many seconds have elapsed since January 1, 1970. (This is a standard for all time functions in most programming languages.) If the user has never logged in, then we save their data as the current time. If the user has logged in, but it has not been twenty-four hours since the last login, they are kicked out of the game.
- Next it waits for the player's avatar to appear in the world, and sets a function that will kick them if they die.

- Lastly, it starts a wait timer for the five minutes we defined earlier. If that timer reaches five minutes, you guessed it: they are kicked. The next function is `OrbWin`. When the player finally gets to the orb, we have conditions that we need to check. If the player has never touched the orb before, we play some happy music, and give them the Orb badge. I won't go into too much detail, because I want you to read through the code to understand what else this function does. Comments kinda give it away. And by the way. Good luck.

The last section of this script is the event connections. We connect the `checkLastLogin` to the `PlayerAdded` event. I connect up the outer portion of the Orb's Touched event to the `OrbWin` function.

MAKING DECISIONS ABOUT YOUR GAME

YOU MAY BE ASKING WHY IN THE WORLD WOULD I KICK PEOPLE OUT OF THE GAME SO MUCH, AND RESTRICT THE AMOUNT OF PLAY TIME, AND MAKE PEOPLE WAIT FOR TWENTY-FOUR HOURS? WELL, IT'S BECAUSE OF WHAT IS HIDDEN IN THE GAME, AND THE FACT THAT I HAVE NEVER SEEN A GAME LIKE IT. I DON'T WANT THE PLAYERS TO BE ABLE TO JUST HOP IN AND GET THE BADGE IN A FEW MINUTES. THIS RESTRICTION FORCES THE PLAYER TO ACT QUICKLY. IT ALSO GIVES A VERY BIG CONSEQUENCE FOR FAILURE. WILL IT WORK? I DON'T KNOW. BUT I AM WILLING TO TRY IT OUT.

FINAL DETAILS

The next script I added into the game was a Music Change. To do this, I added a sphere Part to the entrance of the tunnels.

Roblox Corporation
WE CAN ADD MUSIC TO THIS SPHERE PART.

I made sure that the sphere covered the whole entrance, right-clicked, and added script. I then renamed the script to StartSong. Here's the code I used.

```
canplay = true
this = script.Parent
this.Transparency = 1.0
this.Anchored = true
this.CanCollide = false

this.Touched:Connect(function(part)
    if part.Parent:FindFirstChild("Humanoid") and
    canplay then
        canplay = false
```

```
local player = game.Players:FindFirstChild(part.
Parent.Name)

if player.PlayerGui:FindFirstChild
("BackgroundMusic") then
    music = player.PlayerGui:FindFirstChild
    ("BackgroundMusic")
    for x = 0.5,0.0,-.0125 do
        music.Volume = x
        wait(.1)
    end
    player.PlayerGui.BackgroundMusic:Destroy()
end

Music = Instance.new("Sound",player.PlayerGui)
Music.SoundId = "rbxassetid://1843359148"
Music.Name = "BackgroundMusic"
Music:Play()
  end
end)
```

For the first part we set the transparency to 1.0, and Can-Collide to **false**. This way we can pass through it. When the player touches it, we debounce CanPlay, then check if the user has background music. If they do, we lower the volume slowly with a **for** loop t then start to play our own music.

The next script we have to get up and running is the lever in Chamber 2. Add a script to the LeverHandleUp object. Name the script PullScript. It should look like this:

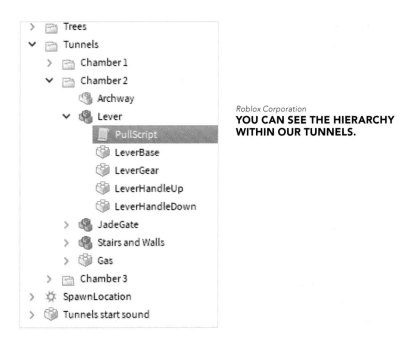

YOU CAN SEE THE HIERARCHY WITHIN OUR TUNNELS.

If you are going to use different names or structures, be sure you know how to find those objects in the script. Here's the code.

```
local this = script.Parent
local pulled = false
local JadeGate = script.Parent.Parent.JadeGate
local leverup = script.Parent.LeverHandleUp
local leverdown = script.Parent.LeverHandleDown

local pull_lever_snd = Instance.new("Sound",this)
pull_lever_snd.SoundId = "rbxassetid://209530691"

local DoorSlam_snd = Instance.new("Sound",this)
DoorSlam_snd.SoundId = "rbxassetid://1843115950"
```

```
leverup.Touched:Connect(function(part)
    if part.Parent:FindFirstChild("Humanoid") and pulled
    ~= true then
        pulled = true
        leverup.Transparency = 1.0
        leverdown.Transparency = 0.0
        pull _ lever _ snd:Play()
        wait(1)
        DoorSlam _ snd:Play()
        wait(.5)
        JadeGate.Parent = nil
    end
end)
```

This script is placed in the Up handle. When the user touches it, we make the Handle Up transparent and we make the Handle Down appear. At the same instance we play a Gear sound that I found in the Roblox library. After waiting for just a moment, we play a Door Slam sound, and make the parent of our Jade Gate **nil**. If an object's parent is not Workspace, then it will not appear.

Our final script will be the gas in this room. (I could have gone further with effects—feel free to take yours up a notch.) Inside the Gas block from earlier, place a script. I named my script DoT for Damage Over Time. The script is quite simple.

```
--damage over time
local CanTouch = true
```

```
script.Parent.Touched:Connect(function(part)
    local hum = part.Parent:FindFirstChild("Humanoid")
    if CanTouch and hum then
        CanTouch = false
        hum.Health = hum.Health - 10
        wait(1)
        CanTouch = true
    end
end)
```

I connect the Touched event to an anonymous function. If the player is touching the block (or walking through it), deal 10 damage, wait for one second, wash, rinse, repeat. Make sure you make this block 1.0 on transparency.

We did it. Finally, we finished with the coding section of the game. Almost. You will need to set your Ambient Light back to 0, 0, 0 so the user cannot see until the Light Spell is cast on them. Make sure that you have your API service enabled so that you can pull DataStores. Past that, I think we have it all covered.

TESTING AND PUBLISHING

Be sure to test your game. Try to find any bugs yourself, then have someone else test for bugs. They may find something you didn't see.

To publish your game so others can play it, navigate to your game in the Create section of Roblox. Just below the game name, you will see an eye icon. The gray eye means the game is private. If you click on it, it will turn green and your game will now be public for all to play.

FINISHING UP

Even after everything is said and done, this is a very, VERY small game. The amount of building, coding, drawing, recording, and other various tasks shows all the different aspects of what goes into games. If you followed along and recreated your own version of this game, I hope it has given you the confidence to make your own games from start to finish!

CHAPTER 10

PROTECTING YOUR GAMES

When you access anything on the internet, you are connecting with people all over the world. Security should always be at the front of your mind, no matter what you're doing. Roblox games are no exception. While most people are in it to have fun, like you are, other people, for whatever reason, will try to cheat, whether through an exploit, a bug, or some other scam. We will be discussing the different ways someone can do harm in your game, what the differences are in each technique, how to secure against them, and what actions to take if your game is compromised.

EXPLOITING VS. HACKING

When we talk about an Exploit, we are talking about someone using an external program that has been written to "inject" code into the game. There are two kinds of injectors:

1. The first is a client that connects to the server just like the Roblox client, but allows you to run Lua script from either a special command bar or a drop-down menu.
2. The second type of exploit is a DLL Injector. When the Roblox client launches, there is a Dynamic Link Library that it uses to process different prewritten function calls. (It's kinda like when we made our own custom functions.) The DLL holds special functions that the client will call. A DLL Injector will change this DLL during runtime, so that when the Roblox client makes a call to a function, the DLL will return the modified function and not the actual function, thus allowing code to be injected into the game.

So why are these methods of interference not called hacking? Isn't an exploit the same thing as a hack? Well, no. Exploiting is not hacking. At least, not in the terms of Roblox games. If you were going to try to hack a Roblox game, you would use some sort of debugger to look at the compiled code of the Roblox client and start working your way backward. This would involve the use of a debug program or a decompiler. Hacking is fundamentally the process of discovering a bug or hole in the security.

Once a vulnerability has been discovered, it is usually made simple by creating a program to use that hack easily and repeatedly. That next step is an exploit. Let's discuss how to stop them.

EXPERIMENTAL MODE

Your first line of defense is to turn off Experimental Mode on your game. (The terminology has changed from Filter Enabled to Experimental Mode.) Experimental Mode is the ability for a client to make a change to their game, which replicates to the server, then replicates to all other clients connected to the server. When Experimental Mode is off, the client cannot make changes to the server except through Remote Events and Remote Functions, which have to be handled by the programmer. When I started writing this book, Experimental Mode was on for all games by default. Now Roblox seems to have changed it for all new games created. It is off by default. This is a good thing. You don't want the clients to be able to make changes without your permission. We will run through some Remote Event examples next.

REMOTE EVENTS AND FUNCTIONS

Both Remote Events and Remote Functions are used to communicate from local scripts to server scripts. Events allow for a single, one-direction communication to happen, while Functions allow for two-way communication. Events are faster than Functions. A Remote Event/Function is a single object. The best practice is to place the Remote Event or Function into the Replicated Storage. Replicated Storage gets copied to both the server and the client. This way both local and server scripts can see them, but can't make changes to them.

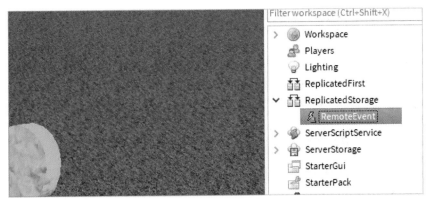

Roblox Corporation
ADDING A REMOTE EVENT.

You should make one Remote Event for every event you want to fire. Do not attempt to set up one event to handle multiple functions in different scripts. Name your event something useful so you can identify it later on. Depending on how many Remotes you use, this list can become very large very quick.

Now, something I have done in the past has been not to name my Remote Events and Functions as what they are intended for, but as a table of references. (It's your choice whether you want to do this too—it sort of helps you protect your game.) For example, I would name an event RE1843, which has no significance, but when I look it up on my list of events that I wrote down, I know that RE1843 is the Remote Event that is triggered when someone touched the Easter egg inside one of my games. The touch was handled by a local script that fires off the RE1843 event, and the server reads off when that event fires.

Let's make a working Remote Event.

- Start by right-clicking on the Replicated Storage and adding in RemoteEvent. Rename the event to PlaceBox.
- Now, find the StarterGui folder, hit the Plus button, and add a ScreenGui. Click the plus next to ScreenGui, and add a Text Button.
- Hit the plus next to the Plus button and add a local script. We will rename the ScreenGui to PlayerGui, the Text Button to PlaceBox, and the local script to ClientPlaceBoxScript.

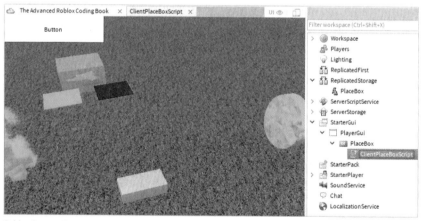

Roblox Corporation
RENAME THE LOCAL SCRIPT AS SHOWN.

Select the PlaceBox Text Button and find the property Text. Change it to "Place a box." Next thing you want to do is add a script to the ServerScriptService. Name the script ServerPlace-BoxScript. We will go ahead and code the ClientPlaceBoxScript first.

```
local RStorage = game:GetService("ReplicatedStorage")
local PlaceBoxEvent = RStorage:WaitForChild("PlaceBox")
local PlaceBoxButton = script.Parent

PlaceBoxButton.MouseButton1Click:connect(function ()
    print("Local Script Fired")
    PlaceBoxEvent:FireServer()
end)
```

We start off this script by creating three variables. The first one uses the **game:**GetService function to get our Replicated Storage. Now we could have used **game.**ReplicatedStorage: and we would have same result. We then use our Replicated Storage to wait for the PlaceBox event. We want to make sure that we use a WaitForChild, because when you are working with Client and Server, there may be a bit of lag or network delay. This ensures that the object will be there when we reference it.

The last thing we need is the button, which our script is sitting in, so we just use a **script.**Parent. (This will not always be the case. You might be creating a big interface of some kind, with multiple buttons.)

Next, I have created an anonymous function for the Place-BoxButton. When the MouseButton1Click event is triggered, we use a **print** to show it has happened, and use the FireServer()

event of the `PlaceBoxEvent` object. Basically, you click the button, fire the event. Now for the ServerPlaceBoxScript.

```
local RStorage = game:GetService("ReplicatedStorage")
local PlaceBoxEvent = RStorage:WaitForChild("PlaceBox")

PlaceBoxEvent.OnServerEvent:connect(function(player)
    print(player.Name .. " just clicked the button")

    local player = workspace:FindFirstChild(player.Name)
    local playerPos = player.HumanoidRootPart.Position

    local NewBox = Instance.new("Part",workspace)
    NewBox.Size = Vector3.new(3,3,3)
    NewBox.Position = playerPos + Vector3.new(0,10,0)
end)
```

Our server-side script is just as simple. We create a variable that points to Replicated Storage, then wait for our `PlaceBox-Event` to show up. Once we have it, we connect an anonymous function that takes in the first variable. When the `ServerEvent` triggers, it will pass the player's name who triggered it. We use this later to get the player's current position in the game. We could use it for many other things, such as getting the player's Backpack items, or changing the user's stats. Now that we have the player, we do a **print** to show who just fired the event. We get the player by searching for the first object in the Workspace that has the same name, using `FindFirstChild`. Next we create a `PlayerPos` variable that looks for the player's `HumanoidRoot-Part` and get its position.

Finally, we create a new instance of a Part inside the Workspace, set the size of that Part to 3×3×3, then set the position to ten units above where the player is, by adding a new **Vector3** to the current `PlayerPos` variable.

Whew! Now we can test it out. When you run the game, you can now click on the button, and make a new Part appear. I had a little fun with mine.

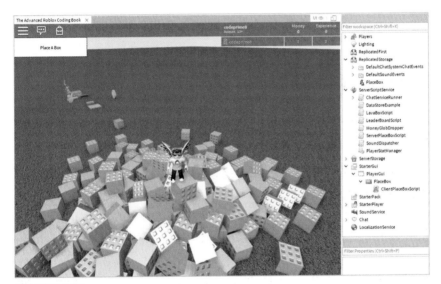

Roblox Corporation
I MADE A BUNCH OF BOXES.

As you can see from the picture, I should put some kind of limit on how many boxes I can create at one time, or put some kind of delay to ensure that I am not spamming the button to create billions of loose Parts at once. Let's move on. Remote Functions work in the same way, except you can get a result from them and pass it back to the script that makes the call.

BE SURE TO CHECK YOUR CALL BACK

BIG WARNING! IF YOU USE A REMOTE FUNCTION INVOKE, AND YOU DO NOT HANDLE THE CALL BACK FOR THAT INVOKE, THEN YOUR SCRIPT WILL NOT CONTINUE TO RUN. THAT MEANS IF YOU CALL AN `Invoke-Server`**, BUT NEVER LISTEN FOR WHAT IT SAYS BACK TO YOU, THEN IT WILL JUST SIT THERE, WAITING, WONDERING WHY YOU DIDN'T PROGRAM IT CORRECTLY. SAD SCRIPT.**

Let's make that call! Start by creating a new Remote Function inside the Replicated Storage, and name it PlaceBoxFunc. Inside our PlayerGui that you already made, we are going to add a new Text Button and name it PlaceBoxFunc. Change its text to "Place A Box – Function". The new Text Button is going to be over the top of the first Text Button. You should be able to just drag it down, so that you can see both buttons.

Roblox Corporation
NOW YOU CAN SEE BOTH BUTTONS.

Add a local script to the button and rename it to ClientPlace-BoxFuncScript. Finally, add a new script to the ServerScriptService, and name it ServerPlaceBoxFuncScript. Overall you added four things and changed some names/properties. Note that we could have done all of this with scripts.

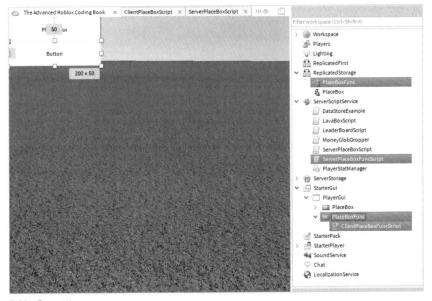

Roblox Corporation
RENAME THE SCRIPTS.

We will start by programming the ClientPlaceBoxFunScript first. Like always, here's the code first, and we'll talk about it afterward.

```
local RStorage = game:GetService("ReplicatedStorage")
local PlaceBoxFunc = RStorage:WaitForChild
("PlaceBoxFunc")
local PlaceBoxFuncButton = script.Parent
```

```
local Red = math.random(0,255)
local Green = math.random(0,255)
local Blue = math.random(0,255)
local myRandomColor = Color3.new(Red,Green,Blue)

PlaceBoxFuncButton.MouseButton1Click:connect(function ()
    local NewPart = PlaceBoxFunc:InvokeServer()
    NewPart.Color = myRandomColor
end)
```

We start by creating our variables. Just like before we have Replicated Storage, Remote Function, and the Button we need to click. But there is something new: I have added `Red`, `Green`, and `Blue` variables. These are assigned a random number from 1 to 255 using the **math.random** function. After that we create a new **Color3** and use these random numbers to generate a random color. We are going to use this to highlight which blocks we created are ours.

Continuing on, we created an anonymous function for when the Button is clicked. Instead of just triggering, like in our event, we have to assign a variable to handle what is returned to our function. We set `NewPart` as the return value of our `PlaceBox-Func:InvokeServer()` command. What happens next is the server will create a box for us, then return that box to us. After we get the box, we change its color locally. Here's the cool part. Only we can see that color on our box. We won't be able to see the colors of the boxes other people create. They will all just look like gray boxes. I know you're excited to test it out, but we have to program the server-side script first. Let's go!

```lua
local RStorage = game:GetService("ReplicatedStorage")
local PlaceBoxFuncEvent = RStorage:WaitForChild(
"PlaceBoxFunc")


function CreateBox(player)
    print(player.Name .. " request a box")
    local NewBox = Instance.new("Part",workspace)
    NewBox.Size = Vector3.new(3,3,3)
    NewBox.Position = Vector3.new(0,10,0)
    return NewBox
end


PlaceBoxFuncEvent.OnServerInvoke = CreateBox
```

We get our PlaceBoxFunctEvent from the Replicated Storage. This time, we are not going to be calling an anonymous function. So instead, we create a function called CreateBox and pass in the player variable. We print the player that wants a box, then create a new instance of a Part, placing it in the center of our game, ten units above 0, 0, 0, and changing the size to 3x3x3. At the end of our function, we call return NewBox. This returns the new Part to the event that's called the invoke. It's up to the local script to handle what to do with it after this. So it's not very different from the event script, except for the way our connection to the function is handled and the return.

Now that you have the scripts in place, we are ready to test it out. But instead of just running the game, which you could do, we are going to use a four-player server. Some computers may have a hard time handling this, so you can do just two if you need.

From the Test menu at the top of the screen, make sure Local Server is selected in the drop-down box, and change the Player box to four Players. Click on Start. You should get four player windows and a server window. In each one of these windows, click on the Place A Box – Function button a few times, and watch what happens.

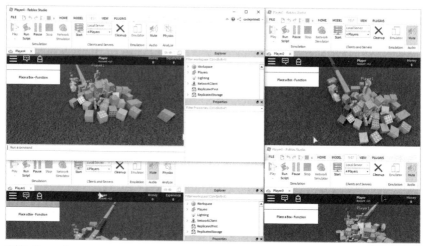

Roblox Corporation

YOU CAN SEE ALL FOUR PLAYERS AT ONCE.

So all the blocks are created on the server, the Part is passed to the client, and the client changes the color. As a result, the color change is only seen by the client, and not the other players or the server. Each player can see their own boxes, but all the other boxes remain the same. This is a GREAT example of how the clients cannot affect the rest of the players.

Now if Experimental Mode was on, or Filtering Enabled off, then these changes would replicate and all the players would see them. These are the main points:

1. Block the client from being able to replicate changes to other clients.
2. Force changes that need to be made to go through a Remote Event or Function.

Now we need to talk about what we can do to prevent the user from doing things on their client that would give them unfair advantages to our game.

COUNTER MEASURES

You should now have a fair amount of knowledge about how to prevent users from affecting other users or the server itself. Keeping Filtering Enabled on and using Remote Events and Functions work to prevent most things, but they can't stop everything. Now we need to worry about what the user can exploit on their end that only affects them. For example, properties like run speed, jump powers, and health. These are all items that are handled on the client side of things. An exploiter can change their properties on their side, and our server wouldn't see the change happen, so we won't be able to use a server script to handle the Anti-Exploits.

This is where everything gets tricky. We are going to have to place a local script onto the player to watch for changes that can occur. If those changes occur, we need to inform the server, and take the appropriate actions to stopping that person. I have a very simple, prebuilt Anti-Exploit script that I built a while back. You can get a copy of it here: www.roblox.com/library/705785509/CodePrime8s-Anti-Exploit-Script-v1-1. It has some good examples of how to prevent exploits on a local level.

HERE'S MY PREBUILT ANTI-EXPLOIT SCRIPT.

Preventing exploits on the client side is good, but here is the next problem. What happens when the local client removes the script? Now we can't check to see if things are being modified. To counteract this, we are going to need to prevent our script from getting removed, either by checking on it with a server script or some other form of detection.

Let's start with a simple local script that will check for jump power, walk speed, and health. (We can add more later.) Create a local script in the StarterPlayer --> StarterCharacterScripts. This will ensure that the script will run every time the player spawns.

Rename your script to AntiCheat. Once you have typed out the code, we will go over what it is doing.

```
local check_interval = 2
local lPlayer = game.Players.LocalPlayer
local oPlayer = game.Workspace:WaitForChild(lPlayer
.Name)

function kickWithMsg(textToShow)
    local MSG = Instance.new("Message",workspace)
    MSG.Text = textToShow
    lPlayer:Kick("Kicked: " .. textToShow)
end


while wait(check_interval) do
    local hum = oPlayer.Humanoid

    --check the Walking Speed. Normal speed is 16
    if hum.WalkSpeed > 16 then
        kickWithMsg("Caught Speed Walking")
    --check the JumpPower. normal is 50
    elseif hum.JumpPower > 50 then
        kickWithMsg("Caught Power Jumping")
    --check if the max health. Normal is 100
    elseif hum.MaxHealth > 100 then
        kickWithMsg("Max Health over 100")
    end
end
```

Let's walk through each section.

- First, we created a `check_interval` variable at the beginning. This will be how often our script will check for changes. We could just set it for every second or wait as long as we want.
- Next, we set the `lPlayer` variable with the local player. Note that the **game**.`Players.LocalPlayer` will only work in local scripts. You cannot use `LocalPlayer` with a server-side script.
- Next, we do a `WaitForChild`, and set our `oPlayer` to the player object that is in the Workspace.

For now, this is all we need to check on settings of the player. Next we create a function called `kickWithMSG` and pass in a single text argument. This is because we want to kick the player every time we find an exploit. You could go further and have a ban list that you would store in the DataStore, but let's keep it simple for now. Next, we set our script into motion by using a while **wait()do** loop. This will make a loop that will wait the amount of time we set at the beginning. Inside the loop, we set a variable called `hum`, and make it point to the player's Humanoid. Now that we can read off all the different properties, we use different **if/then** statements to see if something is higher than the normal range of our properties. If they are, then we initiate a kick, along with the message of why.

That's it! Your simple AntiCheat script is done, and foolproof.

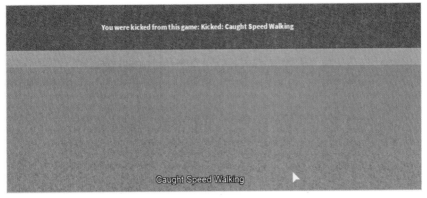

Roblox Corporation
KICKING A PLAYER FOR BREAKING THE RULES.

Ok, ok...you got me. This isn't the only script that we are putting in here.

Like I said, this one is just a simple script to get you started, and give you an idea of what to think about. We will now do a server-side script to check on the local script. You could even make a Remote Function that would check with the local script. If the script doesn't respond, we could assume that something happened to it. Let's make a server-side AntiCheat script.

Place a new script into the ServerScriptService, and name it AntiCheatServer. See if you can figure out what we are doing in the script before I explain it afterward.

```
local check _ interval = 5

function kickWithMSG(player,Message)
    player:Kick(Message)
end
```

```
while(wait(check_interval)) do
    --Get all the players in the game
    local Players = game.Players:GetChildren()
    --Loop through each player
    for key,player in ipairs(Players) do
        --get the players object in world.
        oPlayer = player.Character
        if not(oPlayer:FindFirstChild("AntiCheats")) then
            --if player is missing AntiCheat script, we
            kick them.
            kickWithMSG(player,"AntiCheat local script not
            found.")
        end
    end
end
```

When I released the Anti-Exploit script version 1.1, I never told anyone that I had a server-side script that was working alongside the first script. A lot of exploiters came into my sitting room on Roblox, and would attempt to remove the script from their avatars. I'm pretty sure someone reading this right now is probably going to attempt it as well. I can assure you, my server script is still there and yes, it still works.

To start off, we have the local variable `check_interval` and set it to five. I don't like having a server script run every second because of the amount of traffic Roblox may have at any given time. We create a function just like before called `kickWithMSG` and it takes two arguments:

1. The player we want to kick.
2. The message we want to display after the kick.

Since we are passing in an actual player object, the :Kick function will work. In our main portion of the script, we create an infinite loop that waits five seconds. Inside the loop, we make a `player` variable, and get all the players in the game. Then we loop through all of the players and find their player model in the game. Once we have the player model, we check to see if the AntiCheat script is there. To do this we use an **if not**(oPlayer:FindFirstChild("AntiCheats")) **then** because we want a **false**, and not a **true**. If the script is there, it's an **if not(true)**, which is **false**. That means that it won't run the code inside our **if** statement. But if someone removes the script, it's an **if not(false)** so then we get a **true**, and we run our function kickWithMSG on the player object, and give them the friendly message about not removing our scripts. Now, unless you actually have a way of exploiting and removing the script, there is no way for you to test this. Unless…

Go to the StarterGui script that you created for the Client-PlaceBoxScript (at the beginning of this chapter). You are going to add a line of code to this local script. Right after the `Fire-Server()` trigger, type in the following code.

```
game.Players.LocalPlayer.Character.AntiCheats:Destroy()
```

When you click the button to create a box, you also destroy the AntiCheat script located inside your player model. Publish your game, and test it out on Roblox.

While the kick is nice, if someone is doing this in your game, I still recommend using some sort of ban so they can't come back in. Just my personal opinion.

Roblox Corporation
NOTICE THE KICK MESSAGE.

GOING FURTHER

The scripts I have shown here are simple and basic. They are not intended to stop everyone, and they won't last forever, since Roblox may change things and players might find a way around them. This is just a start. Other items of interest you might look out for are objects being added to the GUI that you didn't put there. A lot of exploits will insert screen GUIs so the user can interact with them.

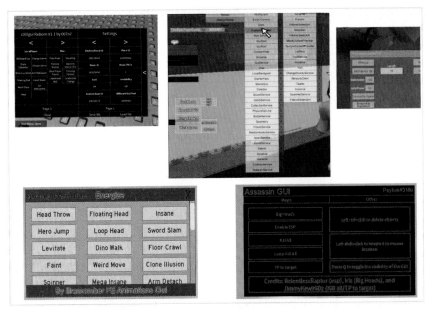

Roblox Corporation

THESE ARE EXAMPLES OF GUIS EXPLOITS MIGHT INSERT.

PUT PLAYERS' BAGS THROUGH A SECURITY CHECK

CHECKING A USER'S INVENTORY AND BACKPACK ARE A GOOD WAY TO PREVENT UNAUTHORIZED ITEMS FROM BEING ADDED INTO THE GAME AS WELL. IF YOUR GAME DOESN'T HAVE GUNS, AND AN AVATAR IS NOW HOLDING ONE, GOOD CHANCES ARE IT GOT THERE THROUGH AN EXPLOIT.

Checking your Remote Events is also a good idea. If the exploiter can see what Remote Events and Functions you have in your Replicated Storage, they could write their own scripts to use these when they wanted.

To stop these, you have to check if there is a client-side script that is running that should not be there. The best way to do this is to have a list of "allowed" scripts, search for all scripts in the client, and if you come across one that is not in the list, it's probably an exploit. (Or you forgot that you had added a script. Or forgot to add that script to the allowed list.)

Security will always be a concern, no matter what type of coding you are dealing with. Because you are going to be programming games, it is my recommendation that you look into how exploits are being used. The Admin in me is screaming, "DON'T TELL THEM THAT," but another voice in me is screaming, "THEY NEED TO KNOW." Sometimes it works best to know what you are up against. The information on how to make exploits is out there. If the "bad guy" can get to them, then so should you. The best way to fight is to know your opponent. I would also like to point out that most exploiters are not really "bad guys," and will happily test your game out for you and help you test the security. They are gamers just like you. Sometimes the best way to protect your game is to have someone you know exploit it.

CONCLUSION

The main point I want you to take away from this book is that programming is fun. There isn't one, and only one, specific way to write every code. You can often change it however you like. I want you to feel confident enough to start writing your own scripts. I want you to create new and exciting games that I can play! If you stumble along the way, I want you to know where to find the answer. Use the scripts in this book as a stepping-stone to help you gain experience and confidence. There is so much more to learn than what I have covered.

Oh, and before I forget, Bloby890, thank you. You were the one who said to record that first video. Without that moment, this book wouldn't exist. To my admins, past, current, and future. Thank you for your help, protection, friendship, and love. Dig-DugPlays, Mumazing, and DarkJ, you said not to forget you if I ever made it big. Does a book count? And to every single fan: You got me here. You made this happen. Thank you.

There are so many other people I want to thank, but I'm pretty sure the editor is freaking out about how much they have to correct in the first place. Keep learning. Never stop. Don't let someone tell you that you can't be something.

Love you all! Thanks for reading!

GLOSSARY

API: Application Programming Interface; a collection of tools for developers.

argument: the data represented by a variable is called its "value." Values are often called "arguments."

CFrame: an invisible frame around an object that designates the object's position and orientation in 3D space.

children: what you see in the Explorer window in Roblox Studio. The "children" include the Workspace, Players, Lighting, and other objects. Each "child" or object you see there can also have its own "children." As in most programs, clicking on the arrow next to the object will expand that object, showing you its children. This parent/child relationship can continue multiple times.

client: the program that allows you to connect to the server.

console output: also called an output box.

DataStoreService: a service for saving information into a Roblox database on their servers.

debounce: to bounce back, as in a variable.

event: a certain thing that occurs at a specific time.

exploit: a malicious program to cheat with.

Explorer window: where you can see everything in your Roblox.

function: a set of instructions that have been grouped together and given a name. Instead of writing the same instructions multiple times, you can group them into a function, then "call" the function to execute those instructions whenever you want.

hack: the process of discovering a bug or hole in the security.

humanoid: a special instance that holds information like Walk-Speed, Health, and JumpPower.

infinite loop: a loop in which a condition is never met and the loop continues to run.

instance: a type of object that has a Parent Class.

key: the number that references a variable inside a table.

kick/kicked: when a player is killed in a game.

local script: a script that runs on a user's client (meaning, on their computer).

logic: the comparison of values, which returns either a true or false statement.

loop: a block of code that will run through all of its instructions, then start back at the top and repeats the same instructions until some predetermined condition is set.

mesh: a 3D object.

method: a special kind of function. Methods perform an action on a variable.

nil: a representation of nothing in coding.

obby: a Roblox game consisting of obstacles for the player to overcome.

pass in: provide; for example, providing data to a variable.

property: an attribution of an part, such as the color, size, name, and position.

Remote Event: used to communicate from local scripts to server scripts. Events allow for a single, one-direction communication to happen.

return: send back, as in the result of a mathematical equation.

script: a set of instructions to perform specific task in a certain way.

server: an instance of the game environment.

server script: a server that runs on the Roblox server that is running the game (meaning, in a remote location).

spawn: regenerate a life for a player.

string: text surrounded by quotation marks. It can contain letters or numbers, usually in words or sentences.

table: used to represent pairs of items. The first item in a pair is called the "index" or "key." The second item in a pair is called its "value." In the example to the left, the keys are types of fruit, and the values are their colors. Tables are declared with brackets, like these: {}.

trigger: specialized events that happen when a certain condition is met.

union: a way to group objects.

variable: a container for some kind of data that is relevant to your game.

vector: a point in the Workspace.

APPENDIX: INFINITE KNOWLEDGE

It's impossible to learn every aspect of scripting. Every day of your journey, you could come across some new line of code, or some different way of doing something. In this section, I'm going to teach you how to teach yourself. That way, if you ever run into a situation that you don't know how to code yet, you'll have a bunch of resources that might have answers for you. Rather than just randomly Googling something, try one of these ideas.

Roblox API page: The first place I want to point out is the Roblox API Index. Remember, API stands for Application Programming Interface. What that means is when we want to create a part, we use an API call that has already been programmed by Roblox.

```
local MyPart = Instance.new("Part",workspace)
```

We do not have to define what an Instance is. We don't program how a Part acts. All of these have been done for us by Roblox, so all we are doing is calling the API functions. Here's a link to API information: http://wiki.roblox.com/index .php?title=API:Class_reference.

The left side of this page will tell you the objects, instances, and services available to you inside Roblox. The center portion of the main page will tell you about the Roblox API and its classes. There is a table of contents on the right-hand side that you can use to navigate to different sections if you would like.

Roblox Corporation
THE API CLASS REFERENCE PAGE.

Let's walk through how to get information on Tools. Scroll down the list until you find the wrench icon with the word Tool beside it, and click on it.

P SelectionPointLasso		1 Class Catego
Guiltem	Classes that are listed here can be created	1.1 3D Int
Backpack	using the Instance.new constructor.	1.2 Adorni
BackpackItem	(However, there are several exceptions, which you might	1.3 Anima
HopperBin	want to be aware of)	1.4 Avatai
Tool		1.5 Consti
Flag	Roblox's API also has several built-in data	1.6 Effects
StarterPack	types, which can be viewed on this page.	1.7 GUI
GuiService	Almost all of the classes here make use of	
HanticCoruico		

Roblox Corporation

LOOK FOR THE TOOL ICON.

Once you have opened up the page, take a moment to just scroll down and look at everything that the page has to offer.

API:Class/Tool

Tool : BackpackItem : Guiltem : Instance

The Tool object acts as a weapon or other object that is stored in a Player's Backpack. When equipped, a tool is automatically transferred to the Player's character and it is held in the right hand by default. Tools require scripting to function, as well as a Part named 'Handle' if the RequiresHandle property is set to 'true'.

Tools are positioned using the grip property.

It is not necessary to use a Tool to capture user input; instead, there are the following alternatives:

- ContextActionService
- UserInputService
- GetMouse method

Properties

[Show hidden members] [toggle]

bool CanBeDropped	If true, when the backspace button is pressed the tool will be parented to the workspace and removed from the player's backpack. If false, when the backspace button is pressed the tool will go back to the Player's Backpack.
bool Enabled	Relates to whether or not the tool can be used.
CFrame Grip	Stores the Tool's Grip properties as one CFrame.
Vector3 GripForward	One of the properties that specifies a Tool's orientation in a character's hand. This represents the R02, R12, and R22 values of the Grip CFrame's rotation matrix.
Vector3 GripPos	The positional offset of a Tool weld matrix.
Vector3 GripRight	One of the properties that specifies a Tool's orientation in a character's hand. This represents the R00, R10, and R20 values of the Grip CFrame's rotation matrix.
Vector3 GripUp	One of the properties that specifies a Tool's orientation in a character's hand. This represents the R01, R11, and R21 values of the Grip CFrame's rotation matrix.
bool ManualActivationOnly	When set to true, the tool will only fire Activated when Activate is called. This also suppresses the ContextActionService's BindActivate function. When set to false, mouse clicks (when the tool is equipped) will also fire Activated.
bool RequiresHandle	If set to false the tool will function without a handle.
string ToolTip	This property controls the message that will be displayed when the player's mouse is hovering over the tool in their backpack.
Content TextureId	The texture that is displayed on a tool in the Player's backpack. If this

Roblox Corporation

THE TOOLS API PAGE.

There is a lot of information on the screen, some you might know, and some you may not recognize. I will highlight the areas and explain what they are and how to use them. Let's look at each part of this image:

- On the top of the Tools API page is the name of what you are looking for and its hierarchy (the green square). It is a child of everything above it, and has some of their properties. These properties are called "inherited."
- Inside the blue box is a description of the API, along with requirements needed to use this object. It will also provide tips on how to use it.
- The purple box usually contains links to other related APIs as they apply. In this case, it's telling us we can use the ContextActionService, UserInputService, and GetMouse to get users' input (instead of using a tool).
- The yellow box contains a list of properties, functions, and events that this class uses.
- In the orange box on the left side is the name of the function, event, or property, along with what it is expecting as input from you, the programmer. Each one of the types is a hyperlink that you can follow to get more information about that type.
- The right-side orange box is a detailed description of what the function, property, or event is and what it can do.

Scroll down a little bit on the page, and find the Activated Event. Because this is an event, it will fire when the user has the tool in hand and clicks the mouse. If you'll look, the "Activated()

word" is a hyperlink that goes to another page. Go ahead and click on it. It will take you to a detailed page of what Activated Event does, and even gives you an example that you can copy and paste into your script if you wanted to test it out.

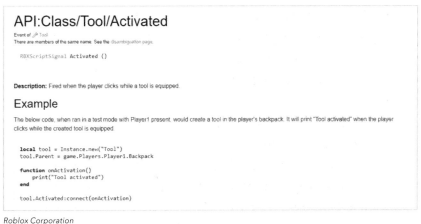

Roblox Corporation

HERE'S AN EXPLANATION OF WHAT THE ACTIVATED EVENT DOES.

The main advantage to the API Class Reference sheet is the fact that you don't need Roblox Studio to look at it. You can access it from your phone, tablet, Chromebook, Wi-Fi toaster, or Xbox One. The other thing I love about this page is that it always contains the latest version of Roblox API.

The Rabbit Hole: What we just looked at was essentially the "pretty" version of the API. Now, let's peek at "The Dump"—a more involved resource.

Go back to the main page of the API Classes (the one that has the instances on the left that you can click). In the middle of the page about four paragraphs from the top, there is a hyper-link called "API Dump." Take a deep breath and click it.

on this page. Almost all of the classes here make use of these data types, such as the Position property of a Part, which uses the Vector3 data type.

If you are looking for information on undocumented classes, one of your best resources is the Object Browser pane (under the Help menu in Roblox Studio). Alternatively, you could look through the API dump itself.

All Game objects are based on Instance and have the "global" methods, properties, and events defined there. Additionally, some classes derive from others, in a hierarchical tree-like structure, shown on the left.

1.5 Constraints
1.6 Effects
1.7 GUI
1.8 Interaction
1.9 Legacy Body
1.10 Lights
1.11 Localization
1.12 Meshes
1.13 Parts
1.14 Post Proces
1.15 Scripting
1.16 Sounds

Roblox Corporation
LOOK FOR THE "API DUMP" HYPERLINK.

What you see before you is the entire list—of all classes, functions, events, enumeration, instances, objects, methods, property—of everything. You should, at this point, be able to read this "dump" file, and understand what each line is talking about. If you find that you are looking for something in the API webpage, and it is not documented, you will most likely have to look it up in the "Object Browser" inside Studio, or travel to this page and see if you can find it. The likelihood of you having to travel here is pretty slim, but I wanted to make you aware of it at the beginning, so you would know what to do. (Personally, I like reading it just for fun!)

The Object Browser: I touched on the Object Browser in the last part of Chapter 4. It is another place where I look up how to create and use objects and services inside Studio. It will be cumbersome at first if you don't know what you are looking for.

To get to the Object Browser, go to the View menu at the top of the screen inside Studio, and click on the Object Browser button at the top. API items are on the left. When you click one, Properties, Functions, Events appear on the right. Select one of them to view details at the bottom.

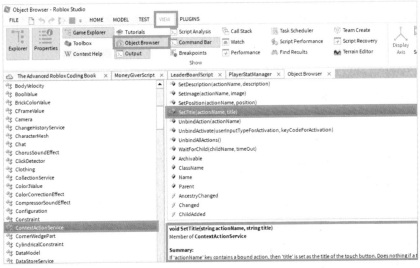

Roblox Corporation

THIS SHOWS YOU THE OBJECT BROWSER OPTIONS.

The Object Browser is the quickest way to find something you know you are looking for. It's very targeted, and direct in what you need to use an API. This is always current since it updates every time Studio does.

Roblox Dev: Roblox has done a really great job of gathering a lot of resources into one place, called Developer, and you can get to it from this link: http://robloxdev.com/. Here, you can look up APIs, search tutorials, and ask questions from the community. I have used this page in a few of my own YouTube videos, walking through the lessons, and teaching step-by-step what the pages are communicating.

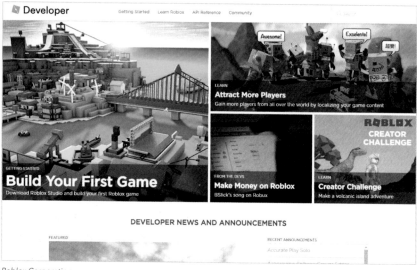

Roblox Corporation
ROBLOX DEVELOPER PAGE.

I recommend combing this site. Start with the Getting Started section on the top left. This section is going to walk you through a simple obby. It is like the introduction section to Roblox Studio.

Roblox Corporation

THIS GIVES YOU LOTS OF INFORMATION ON WRITING AN OBBY.

At the bottom of the tutorial, it will make suggestions and recommendations on what to try and where to go next. In the next section of the page, you'll see "Learn Roblox," which has categories of materials on the left-hand side and the actual materials on the right-hand side. Each one is categorized into Articles, Videos, Recipes, and Code Samples. This page allows you to find things pretty quickly but doesn't cover everything you might be looking for. It's a great system to use when you are experimenting with something new.

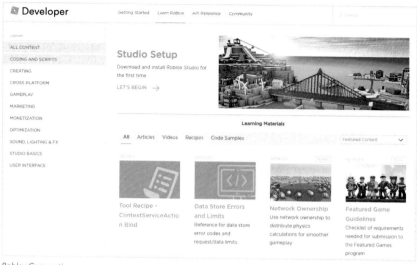

Roblox Corporation

THIS LEARN ROBLOX WINDOW HAS A LOT TO OFFER.

Ah, look at that. There's the link for the API Reference. Right? Not exactly. The next link, API Reference, does not take you to the same section we looked at in the beginning of this section. This API Reference is set up differently. It has the categories on the left... But wait—it has two portions: the Type Index Pages and the Class Categories. This allows you to break down each API by what you are looking for. There is also a Search function that allows you to quickly find sections that contain keywords that you are looking for. Take a moment to try out the search by typing in Body. It will narrow your categories down to Avatar and Body Movers.

Roblox Corporation
THE REFERENCE MANUAL.

The last portion of the Roblox Developer page is the Community. This link will take you over to the Roblox devforum, https://devforum.roblox.com/. That's where developers ask questions, seek answers, and communicate with fellow developers. It is very rare to ask a question that has not been asked already. Not that it can't happen, but if you are having an issue in Studio, most likely someone has already had the same problem, and it has already been answered. First search for your topic before posing a new question. If you are registered and logged in, you can also track articles as they change, and get notifications for any news about a thread.

Roblox Corporation

HERE'S THE DEVELOPER FORUM.

Like I said, Roblox has done a great job of putting information out there for us developers to explore. Use the site. Practice the tutorials. I promise, it will become second nature, and you will get better at creating.

YouTubers: Sometimes, watching someone work through a process is helpful too. YouTube gives many creators the freedom to look up tutorials and follow along, creating various things inside Roblox. I have created tutorials on how to script, program, and make various things on Roblox, in Lua, and in Studio. You can find my channel at www.youtube.com/user/CodePrime8. I play

Lumber Tycoon 2 mostly, but have various other tutorial videos that you can watch.

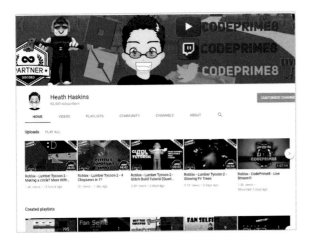

Roblox Corporation
MY ROBLOX CHANNEL.

There is also someone I believe deserves a special shout-out: AlvinBLOX. His videos on Roblox scripting are very well made, and have been around since I started Roblox. Thanks, Alvin, for the hours of entertainment and education. You rock!

Roblox Corporation
ALVINBLOX'S YOUTUBE CHANNEL.

There are many more great Roblox YouTubers out there who make great content. I won't list them all, but I would like to show you how to search YouTube to find them. If you are just looking for tutorials, use keywords such as Tutorial, Lua, Roblox, Studio, How-To, and Walkthrough. Keeping the phrasing simple helps to narrow down searching. For example, let's say I needed to learn how to create a new gun for my game. If I search "How do I create a new sword for my game?" I'm not going to get what I was looking for.

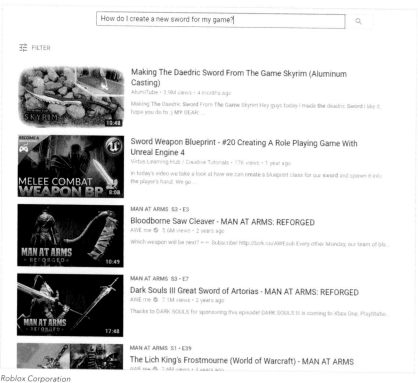

Roblox Corporation
THIS SWORD SEARCH ISN'T USEFUL..

Now, by using the keywords, and phrases properly, we can narrow our search down and get what we are looking for. Change the search to "How to Make Sword Roblox Lua" and you will get a very different result.

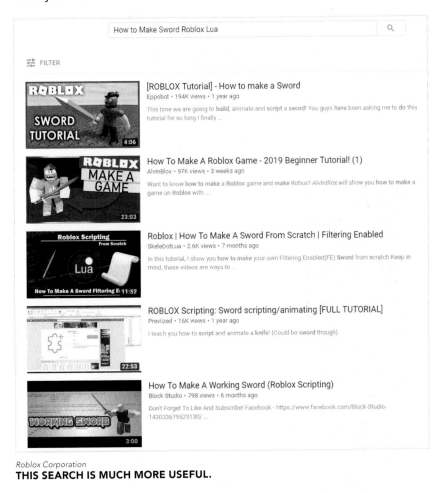

Roblox Corporation
THIS SEARCH IS MUCH MORE USEFUL.

Once you have your search results, know that it's not always the first video that is going to give you the answer. You might not even find it on the first page. Here are a few aspects of videos that you should look for when you are trying to find tutorials:

- Did the creator use a microphone? This is the number one thing that makes me close a video and stop watching. You should be able to hear them clearly.
- Does the creator type in the video? For me, when someone opens up a notepad and starts typing inside a video, I move on. I want to "watch" a video, not "read" a video.
- Is the creator knowledgeable on the subject? Did they just copy and paste their code or are they typing it out as they go?
- How is the overall quality of the video? This is a personal preference. If someone has done a really good job at presenting the code, demonstrating how it works, and walking through the process, then I am okay with a 480p resolution. But you might prefer videos with better effects and such.

Keep Learning: Nicely done! You've come a long way. Remember, your overall success of the Lua programming language is not going to be defined by how much you know off the top of your head. Knowing where to go to find the answer you are looking for is going to be more important. Continue learning, continue practicing, and keep getting better.

INDEX